IMMIGRATION CROSSROADS

THE MACMILLAN COMPANY
NEW YORK · BOSTON · CHICAGO · DALLAS
ATLANTA · SAN FRANCISCO

MACMILLAN & CO., LIMITED
LONDON · BOMBAY · CALCUTTA
MELBOURNE

THE MACMILLAN CO. OF CANADA, LTD.
TORONTO

IMMIGRATION CROSSROADS

BY
CONSTANTINE PANUNZIO, Ph.D.

PROFESSOR OF SOCIAL ECONOMICS,
WHITTIER COLLEGE

The great question is to discover,
not what governments prescribe,
but what they ought to prescribe;
for no prescription is valid against
the conscience of mankind.
          —*Lord Acton.*

NEW YORK
THE MACMILLAN COMPANY
1927

TO

LENORE

WIFE AND COMRADE

FOREWORD

This book aims to set forth in broad outlines America's significance to the laborer of the Old World, the contributions immigrants have made to the development of the United States, the changes in the attitude of the people of this country toward immigration, certain aspects of a possible constructive immigration policy and the international phase of the migration movement and of our restriction policy. Whatever its merits, it is the product of years of contact with immigrant groups, of study and thought upon the immigration problem and of nearly two years close observation and attentive listening in the legislative halls at Washington.

I have sought to present a readable, frank and fair interpretation of relevant facts. In writing it I have kept in mind the thoughtful citizen, the constructive-minded legislator, the employer of labor, the student of population and labor problems, the Americanization worker and those interested in international and inter-racial questions. I have purposely made the work simple and direct. I have avoided, for the most part, footnotes and bibliographical references since in many cases they would have occupied nearly as much space as the text and would have made the work cumbersome without adding particularly to its usefulness.

As an adopted American I have naturally, perhaps unavoidably, stressed the immigrant's point of view of the whole matter. I hope, however, that this will only enhance whatever value the work may possess, since most contemporary writing on immigration stresses the other side of the case. If at any point this book appears to be turning simply into an argument against restriction it will be due to some unhappy turn of phrase. The reader is kindly asked to suspend his judgment, to go on and get the spirit of the whole, since I have aimed to present not an argument, but an honest and frank analysis.

I acknowledge my indebtedness to the Robert Brookings Graduate School of Economics and Government, Washington, D. C., for having granted me a fellowship which made it possible for me to spend nearly two years in research work and observation in Washington; portions of this work were submitted to that School in partial fulfillment of its requirements for the degree of Doctor of Philosophy. I am also indebted to the *Standard* for permission to reproduce the last chapter, to Miss Edythe Johnson for invaluable assistance in the correction of the proofs, and to my wife for unfailing encouragement.

C. P.

Whittier, Calif.
June 1, 1927

CONTENTS

IMMIGRATION CROSSROADS

IMMIGRATION CROSSROADS

CHAPTER I

THE LABORERS' NEW WORLD

Whence came all these people! They are a mixture
of English, Scotch, Irish, French, Dutch, Germans
and Swedes. From this promiscuous breed that race
now called Americans has arisen. . . . Here individuals of all nations are melted into a new race of
men, whose labors and posterity will one day cause
great changes in the world. Americans are the western pilgrims, who are carrying along with them that
great mass of arts, sciences, vigor and industry which
began long since in the east; they will finish the great
circle.—*de Crèvecour.*

I

WHEN Columbus chanced upon the New World
little did he foresee, nor could he have foreseen, what
his discovery would mean to the working classes of
the Old World. For several centuries the worker had
led a life which to all intents and purposes was
narrow and cruel, degraded and degrading. He was
tied politically, socially and economically to the
very spot and conditions in which birth had set him.
Governments took an interest in him principally as
a tool of warfare. His masters owned him, had

1

the right to purchase or sell him, import, export and exploit him at will. He was forced to work on the land of a given proprietor whether he wished to do so or not. He had to take his grain to the seignior's mill to be ground, his bread to be baked in the master's ovens and his vintage to be made into wine only at his lord's winepress. If he committed an offense, it was to his seignior that he had to pay a fine; if he perpetrated a crime, the owner condemned him to death and confiscated his possessions such as they were. He had no right to assemble with his fellows, even to consider his own affairs. He could not marry or give his children in marriage without the permission of his seignior, nor could he choose his own burial place. The lord sat in judgment and rendered verdicts involving life and death. In short, if the records coming down to us are at all trustworthy, it appears that the laborer of the Middle Ages was deprived of every right and privilege which we now consider the birthright of the most ordinary person, and no amount of personal merit or industry, aspiration or discontent could possibly raise him above the state to which the accident of birth had assigned him.

The laborer's lot was even more difficult because his world was stagnant and limited. Population was practically stationary, trade nearly at a standstill. The pressure of population on the land and food supply was quite complete. Food was scarce and poor in quality. Chronic hunger hung upon the masses like a shadow. Devastating famines and plagues raged like flames, swept sections of entire countries, at times destroying as many as one-third of a nation's population.

But what could the worker do about the matter? He had reached the very rim of the then known world. To the west lay only the Atlantic and beyond it nothing but a vague and vast abyss. Under such conditions he could do nothing but resign himself to his fate. Energy, therefore, was lacking, lethargy and apathy hung like a pall upon men and a hopelessness of spirit seems to have been quite general and complete.

It is not difficult to imagine what it meant to that torpid, decaying society when the Genoese Navigator brought the news, early in 1493, that he had found a New World. Naturally no one at first could realize the full import of that discovery, and yet it seems as if from the very first the masses were stirred by the news. Herrera in his *General History* tells us how the Admiral gained a "wonderful reputation" among the common people. More's *Utopia* and Montaigne's writings reflect the hope which America's discovery seems to have awakened among the humbler classes. In time, as the news of the discovery spread, it seemed to shake them out of their stupor. Their gaze, thus far centered on the Mediterranean, now turned outward. Their imagina-

tion took sudden leaps, their outlook broke the bonds
of inland seas and "the ports of the shore of the
Atlantic were no longer outposts on the bounds
of a waste estranging sea, but outlets toward a vast
New World."

II

Government representatives, commercial enterprises and the privileged were the first to set out
for the New World. And this was natural. America
was believed to be a sort of storehouse of wealth
to be seized and held. So the rulers of the Old World
hastened to dispatch their cohorts to stake claims.
The early years saw a veritable host of adventurers
and seekers after gold and silver setting out for the
New World. The Spanish consisted, for the most
part, of functionaries of the Spanish Government,
impoverished aristocrats and idlers of every sort,
who were goaded on by a desire to live in luxury
and ease. But they abused rather than utilized the
splendid opportunities of the New World and pro-
voked bitter dissent at home and strife among the
natives.

The French, on the other hand, were dominated
primarily by the desire to establish trading posts.
They depended chiefly upon the sword. Their
colonies, modeled after Old France, were ruled by an
iron hand. A paternalistic régime and an exacting
ecclesiastical discipline prevailed. Their colonies,

therefore, were but the nursling of the parent state, teeming with lawless elements, who explored, exploited and traded in order to establish French sovereignty. And since, as Lecky observes in this very connection, "dominion acquired by the sword can only be maintained by the sword" the French Colonies degenerated into military-ridden centers and so were dwarfed and stunted practically out of existence.

A century and a half passed and government functionaries, commercial enterprisers and privileged proprietors, all alike, faced a blank wall of failure. The New World baffled them. It refused to submit to swords or regal splendors, adventurers and explorers. It repeatedly sent the would-be conquerors back to the Old World with remembrances only, memories of shattered hopes, squandered fortunes and "lost" colonies. And for all intents and purposes America was almost as much of a vacuity in the first decades of the seventeenth century as it had been previous to its discovery.

III

From the very first the English colonies seem to have differed from the others. In the first place, they were *private* enterprises, legalized by government charters. Again, they devoted their energies chiefly to social, political and economic development rather than to mere aggrandizement. Early in the seventeenth century English enterprisers appear to have realized that what they needed above all else was *workers*, if they were to win the New World.

For many years, their effort seems to have been directed almost entirely toward securing laborers. They established recruiting stations in the mother country at first, and later on the continent. They offered inducements of various kinds such as free land, aids in surveying and plotting, security and guarantee of title, free tools and implements and the privileges of citizenship. They paid premiums to owners and masters of vessels who would bring about the actual settlement of workers in the colonies.

Nor did it matter where the workers came from or by what means they were secured, so long as they did come. Virginia, for example, Max Farrand observes in *The Development of the United States*, was "willing to accept settlers" of any sort and on any terms, and "the need was so great, especially for labor, that compulsion was resorted to." Fiske records that "When the prisons in England were encumbered with criminals, a clearance was sometimes effected by sending shiploads of them to Virginia to be sold into slavery for a term of years. Gypsies, vagabonds, and orphans were kidnaped and disposed of in the same way."

So keen was the desire to secure workers that a sharp competition developed between the various proprietors and colonies, and by offering superior inducements some colonies succeeded not only in securing larger numbers of settlers from the Old World, but also in attracting considerable numbers from neighboring settlements.

The news of this demand for laborers in the New World soon spread among the masses of western Europe and met with eager response. Large numbers of workers began to come as indentured servants, selling themselves into practical servitude for the privilege of liberating themselves from Old World conditions, and of coming to the New World.

The beginning of the great migration was on. While the French and Spanish colonies dwindled down to ineffective centers, the English settlements grew rapidly in population, power and prestige. In 1600 there were practically no settlers in the region later occupied by the United States. Twenty years later they numbered 2500; twenty years after that, 25,000; in 1700 (estimate) 250,000; by the middle of the 18th century about one million; and by 1790, the date of the First United States Census, nearly four millions.

They came from almost every principal country of western Europe. Driven by poverty and tyranny in their parent countries and drawn by the call of the New World, English and French, Germans and Swedes, Welsh, Scotch and Irish and Dutch poured into the North American colonies, turned them into beehives of new life and laid the foundations of a new and progressive nation.

IV

As the colonies grew, however, the early settlers developed certain attitudes regarding the admission of newcomers, and adopted definite criteria for the admission of immigrants. *Religious belief* was one of the first and perhaps the most widely adopted method of selection. Persons not agreeing in religious matters with those already in the colony were rejected. Massachusetts discouraged and even prohibited the entrance of non-Puritans. Virginia admitted only those belonging to the Church of England and for a number of years actually debarred non-Conformists. Virginia, also, together with all the New England colonies, except Rhode Island, prohibited the entrance of Quakers. Up to the middle of the Eighteenth Century, moreover, most of the colonies imposed all kinds of restrictions upon the coming of Catholics, varying from absolute prohibition in the Puritan colonies to the petty regulations and annoyances practised by the middle colonies.

Workers seeking admission were selected in other ways. *Strangers*, that is persons unknown by someone already in a colony, were considered undesirable. The New England colonies imposed heavy fines upon those who introduced people into the colonies without permission from the authorities. *Poor persons,*

or those not having enough to start life on without
the aid of the old settlers, were also practically
debarred. *Criminals* and *paupers* were later singled
out. As early as 1722 a head tax was laid upon
criminals landed in the colonies. Ship owners were
also quite generally held accountable for importing
paupers.

In one colony at least, Pennsylvania, an attempt
was made to *restrict* the number of those to be
admitted. That colony, which from the very first
pursued a generous policy of admission, found itself
so overrun by Germans that in 1725 the authorities
began to evince concern lest the "province" should
"degenerate into a foreign colony", foreign in speech
and manners, and thereby endanger the "Quiet of our
adjacent Colonies." Accordingly, a law was passed
in 1829, which, considering the time, was very
drastic: it imposed a head tax of forty shillings on
all foreigners, that is, non-English, who sought
admission to the colony. The law, however, was in
force only for a few months and therefore played no
important part.

V

Difficult as it is to trace cause and effect it seems
quite clear that these varying practices had some
influence in producing (1) a segregation of settlers
by nationality, (2) a difference in the rate of population growth, and (3) sharply differing attitudes

and culture in the various sections. New England and Virginia came to be occupied almost exclusively by the English, while the middle colonies, notably New York and Pennsylvania, came to be inhabited by peoples of several nationalities. And this in turn seems to have set a stamp upon the character, the temper and the outlook of the three sections, differences which have persisted to this day and have played some part in the history of the United States.

Massachusetts, for instance, became predominantly English, primarily on account of its policy of excluding all non-Puritans. Church membership was the measuring rod of fitness. The Puritans refused admission "to the freedom of this body politic" to anyone not a member of "some of the churches within the limits of the same." Only Puritans then could be admitted. And since the Puritans were English it followed that only Englishmen could live in Massachusetts. So vigorously was this policy carried out that for many years that colony remained exclusively Puritan and English; and not only kept out practically all non-English people, but also expelled many English persons, some of whom, such as Roger Williams, Wheelwright, Mrs. Ann Hutchinson, Thomas Hooker and their followers went to the adjacent colonies, while thousands returned to England.

In the Dutch settlements an entirely different situation developed. The Dutch were a people advanced "in the modern pursuits of trade and commerce." Like all traveled and commercial people they were kindly disposed toward all peoples, whatever their "race" or nationality, religious or political belief. They, therefore, remarks Fiske, in *The Discovery and Colonization of North America,* "pursued a policy of toleration and hence, in that cruel age of religious turmoil, they drew settlers from almost every country in Europe." As a result New Netherlands became a cosmopolitan colony. In the city of New Amsterdam on Manhattan Island, with only about fifteen hundred inhabitants in 1640, people of eighteen different nationalities lived side by side peacefully. The same situation obtained in the entire Dutch settlement. Governor Horatio Seymour pointed out that nine men prominent in New York State's early history represented the same number of nationalities. Crèvecoeur said of the people of New York (and Pennsylvania), "They are a mixture of English, Scotch, Irish, French, Dutch, Germans, and Swedes. . . . I could point out to you a family whose grandfather was an Englishman, whose wife was Dutch, whose son married a French woman and whose present four sons have now four wives of different nations." In this manner the foundations of a cosmopolitan New York were laid.

Pennsylvania also became the home of a varied and tolerant people. In the development of this colony William Penn adopted the two principles of

religious freedom and sound business; and to these
the colony adhered quite consistently throughout
its early history. "Never was a colony founded upon
more liberal principles," observes Fiske. "Absolute
freedom of conscience was guaranteed to every one,
the laws were extremely humane, and the land was
offered to immigrants on very easy terms."

People of different "races" and nationalities,
religious and political beliefs flocked to Pennsylvania. English Quakers, German Pietists, Men-
nonites, and Catholics; Scotch and Irish Presby-
terians and French Huguenots found in it a hospit-
able home. Some were wealthy, but the majority were
poor. They came in search of the privilege of leading "a quiet, godly and honest life in a howling
wilderness." Escaping a world of intolerance and
inhospitality, they craved for nothing else than
a chance to work and live. And Pennsylvania did
not fail them. They were not only permitted to
enter freely but were actually *welcomed* into the City
of Brotherly Love and the territory of the Holy
Experiment.

The colony grew rapidly in numbers and leadership. "Within three years from its foundation,"
Fiske records, "Pennsylvania contained eight thousand inhabitants, and it was not long in outgrowing
all the other colonies except Virginia and Massachusetts. Of the white population scarcely half
were English; about one-third were Germans and

the remainer chiefly Irish. In 1776 Philadelphia
was the largest city in the United States, with a
population of thirty thousand, and in literary
activity and general culture it was second only to
Boston." And Pennsylvania became the most cosmopolitan of all colonies, New York not excepted.

Maryland was founded by Lord Baltimore for the
purpose of providing a home of tolerance for himself and his followers, a privilege which Virginia
had denied to them. The leaders were mostly
Roman Catholics, but the majority of the settlers
were Protestants. In general a policy of tolerance
was pursued. And as in the case of New York and
Pennsylvania, this policy "soon began to draw men
of all creeds to Maryland, and the colony grew
rapidly in population and wealth" much to the
jealousy and indignation of neighboring Virginia.

Virginia became almost exclusively English. In
this colony not only the policy of religious exclusiveness prevailed, but also a system of land owner-
ship which was bound to produce segregation. The
Virginian proprietors established a replica of the
English manorial system, in which only the lord and
the lorded had a place. Freemen, of course, would
not submit to such a régime, since they had left the
Old World to escape precisely such conditions; the
pages of colonial history abound with interesting
and significant evidence of the freemen's struggle
against the masters. Virginia consequently was

obliged to draw its workers from those classes who were willing or were compelled to submit to quasi slavery. And since these could be obtained only by compulsion and since the more or less coercive recruiting of laborers could only be possible on English soil, it followed that both Virginian lords and Virginian serfs were for the most part English—barring the Negroes, of course. As the result of this combination of forces Virginia was inhabited almost entirely by the English and by a lower grade of that people.

Of the other colonies just a word will suffice. North and South Carolina were founded much on the order of Virginia. However, in both these colonies the influence of the Conformists was not so great, consequently large numbers of French Huguenots, Germans, Swiss and Scotch-Irish gradually drifted in. In South Carolina more than half the population was of this element; in North Carolina the proportion was also considerable although not so great. The Quakers, treated with inhospitality everywhere except in Rhode Island and Pennsylvania, settled in part of New Jersey, which, for a time, they owned.

By the time of the First United States Census, 1790, the distribution of population by nationality groups stood as follows. The population of the United States in that year numbered four millions, in round numbers. Of these two and a half million

were English, about two-thirds of whom were concentrated in two states: Virginia and Massachusetts,
the very states in which, as we have seen, rigid
exclusiveness had been practised. In Virginia ninety-
four per cent of the population was English. New
England as a whole was nearly as English as Old
England. In Maine over ninety-three per cent of the
population was English; in Massachusetts ninety-
five, in Vermont a little over ninety-five per cent.
Only one other state had as large a proportion
of English and that was Rhode Island (96.0), where
non-Puritan English had taken refuge.

In nonexclusive Pennsylvania, on the other hand,
not only large numbers of English found their
homes, but here also resided three-fourths of the
175,000 Germans, one-fourth of all the Scotch and
large numbers of Irish and other national groups.
Four-fifths of all the Dutch in the United States in
1790 were in the zone of tolerance: New York, New
Jersey and Pennsylvania. What few Jews there
were lived almost entirely in New York and Maryland. The largest single group of Irish were living
in New Jersey, the very state in which there were
the fewest English.

VI

What this segregation of national groups on the
one hand, and their commingling on the other, meant
is apparent at least in part in the sectional attitudes
which developed and which have persisted to this

day. The South as a whole became the center of the one-"race" idea in which only the people of a given "race" had any right to live, rule and direct the affairs of men. The Civil War and other "racial" conflicts have had their principal roots in the South. "Race" relations have always been strained in that region. That section gave birth to and was the defensive stronghold of the Know Nothing and the All American movements and of the first and second Ku Klux Klan; and in these latter days the South has been the leader in the fight against scientific thought. In art, literature and scientific discovery it has also been comparatively unproductive.

New England, notably Massachusetts, on the other hand, yielding to the pressure of the success enjoyed by the less exclusive colonies, gradually and reluctantly gave way to the inrush of "races", and has, in many respects, become quite progressive. But New England, to this day still bears the marks of early intolerance. If the Pope does at present "rule Massachusetts", as some believe, it may be due at least in part to that very early intolerance. Moreover, this papal supremacy, real or imaginary, desirable or undesirable as it may be, represents but an extension of the principle followed by early Massachusetts, for newcomers are but adopting the tactics of the colonists in carrying their religion and religious allegiances to the polls.

Nor is it difficult to perceive how far reaching an influence the zone of tolerance (New York, New Jersey and Pennsylvania) has had upon the life of this country. That zone from the first day to this has been the heart of industry and commerce which have made the United States preëminent among modern nations. It offered an opportunity to peoples of all "races", nationalities, religious and political beliefs, and these rewarded it with an industry and a frugality which has made that section the center of the nation's wealth. Moreover, the "gracious and free and broadly tolerant" life the Dutch led and permitted others to lead, their establishment in 1621 of a free educational system, their advocacy of the free ballot and their founding of New York— all have left a deep and lasting impress upon the nation which, "good" or "bad" as it may ultimately prove to be, has nevertheless been one of the most potent forces directing the destinies of America.

VII

All these facts and movements have a deeper and more lasting meaning. They represent the struggle of the worker to free himself from the stifling conditions of a decaying world and to establish a veritable New World. Wherever they came from, whatever their "race" or nationality, their religion or political belief, all they asked for was a place where they could work and a chance to gain by toil a life which the Old World had refused to yield them. And it was that work that accomplished what government functionaries had failed to do by swords and regal splendors. These "slaves of toil, with hearts of yearning" felled the forests, plowed the fields, opened harbors, penetrated rivers, scaled mountains and blazed the trails far into the interior which opened up the New World. In the opportunity to work even the humblest newcomers found a new lease of life. And their work laid the foundations of the new and progressive nation of the West.

And when this aspect of United States history is fully written it will become even clearer than it is to-day that herein lies the deeper significance of the migration movement from the Old to the New World. The day when the New World opened its arms to the workers was indeed a new day, a turning point in the history of the laborer himself and in the history of man the world over. The worker rose to new dignity on American soil and America itself grew great with that dignity. And each paid the debt to the other, until one day the Old World worker met America full grown at the crossroads and a conflict ensued. . . . those who had come first had forgotten and that may make a great difference. . . . may lead to another turning point in the history of man.

CHAPTER II

THE ASYLUM OF ALL THE WORLD

There's freedom at the gates and rest
For earth's down-trodden and opprest,
A shelter for the hunted head,
For the starved laborer toil and bread.—*Bryant.*

[Here the] free latch-string never was drawn in
Against the poorest child of Adam's kin.—*Lowell.*

I

THE Declaration of Independence, then, may well be looked upon as a landmark in the history of the working classes. The settlers had succeeded in opening up a new continent and in defeating, at least in part, efforts to reëstablish an old order in the New World. They now declared themselves independent and set out on a road of their own.

How far the makers of the new country were conscious of the part immigration had played in the making of their nation may be gathered from the interesting fact that both the Declaration of Independence and the Constitution make mention of the subject. In the former the colonists declared that one of their chief grievances was that the government of the mother country had hindered the free flow of workers into the colonies. And the Constitution states that "the migration or importation of such persons as any of the States now existing shall think proper to admit shall not be prohibited by Congress prior to the year one thousand eight hundred and eight. . . ." (Article 1, Sec. 9.)

The birth of the Union released these restraints and at the same time brought into existence new forces and conditions which were bound to stimulate migration; and for fully a century the great migration went on practically without hindrance. When the consciousness of nationality and independence dawned with full force upon the people and they realized something of the size of the territory and the ease with which they could acquire land, it seems as if the whole youthful nation started moving. New England war veterans secured one million acres of western lands and led the way; New York financiers purchased five million acres and encouraged peoples to migrate; daring spirits like Daniel Boone blazed trails into the interior; the Mississippi Valley was opened for settlement in 1785; vast tracts of land were thrown open by the government in 1800 and 1820 and enormous areas were put on sale by land speculators who vied with the government in selling more cheaply and in smaller acreage.

The love of adventure, also, the lure of the wilderness, the call of the wild, the appeal of nature in

its pristine beauty, each added its stimulus. And
men followed. Waving care-free farewells, they left
their abodes and turned their expectant faces toward
the West. As Channing puts it, they experienced
"no feelings of affection for houses and lands they
left behind; they only looked to the future and
over the mountains and rivers to the westward."
(*The History of the United States.*)

Hard upon the wilderness invaders came the farming and planting pioneers, led by the desire for
economic betterment. "They exhibited some symp-
toms of settled existence, building better cabins than
the half-faced camps. They cultivated the fields
for several years until the ground was free from
stumps, the soil pulverized, and neighbors appeared.
Then the 'Western Fever' seized upon them and
drove them once more to the wilderness:—to the
Connecticut River, to New York State, to the
Western Reserve, to Illinois, to Minnesota and
beyond." (Channing.)

A veritable human stream! For a few there
was the thrill of exploration, for hundreds the lure
of adventure, for the thousands the incentive of a
new economic opportunity. With resistless and
feverish haste they marched westward, breaking the
bounds of mountain barriers, opening the gates to
immense interiors, and as they marched they were
but blazing the way for a still greater inrush of
population.

So great was the emigration from the Atlantic seaboard that at times it threatened to depopulate whole sections of the East. Everyone, it seems, was "going West". "In 1820, the western population, instead of being less than half a million as it would have been by the usual excess of births over deaths, was over two and a half millions; at least one million and a half of this increase represented immigrants from the older states. In the second thirty years from 1820 to 1850, the inhabitants of Transappalachia more than doubled by some five millions; the seaboard section, notwithstanding the great immigration from Europe in the last ten years of that time failing to double by at least two millions. It would seem probable, therefore, that in those two decades, the West took at least four million people out of the East." (Channing.)

II

The news of this extraordinary movement must have spread rapidly in Europe, for people seemed fairly to dash across the ocean, to pass through the East out into the Great West. Out of troubled England, newly-awakened Scandinavia, oppressed Germany and starving Ireland poured the humbler classes and into this country in ever increasing numbers.

Figures give some idea of the steady widening of this human stream: about 250,000 (estimate)

between 1776 and 1819; 150,000[1] between 1820 and
1830; nearly 600,000 in the next decade; almost
1,750,000 in the following ten-year period; and
2,500,000 between 1851 and 1860. Five and a
quarter millions, then, arrived between 1776 and
1860.

By far the larger proportion of these incoming
thousands went to the West. "Of the immigrants
who came in the years before 1850," Channing com-
putes, "about one-half . . . remained in or near the
port of debarkation." A few of the newcomers
sought the Far South, but the great mass of those
who did not stay on the northern seaboard could
be found in the Old Northwest and in the country
just across the Mississippi. Ninety-five per cent
went into the North and the West, avoiding the
states of slave labor. A Southerner complained that
"Every winter considerable numbers of Germans,
Swiss and Scotch arrived in Charleston, with the
avowed intention of settling among us, but are soon
induced to emigrate toward the West, by perceiving
most of the mechanical arts performed by free persons of color."

III

In the meantime someone here and there began
to raise his voice against the incoming stream.
Jefferson, for instance, wrote upon the subject as

[1] Figures in round numbers.

early as 1788. He favored the admission of trained artisans, he said, but opposed the free admission of agricultural or general laborers. The reason he gave was indeed curious. They come from monarchial countries, he argued. That being so, they will "either inject the monarchical principle into America's Republic or they will go to the other extreme of unbounded licentiousness. . . . It would be a miracle if they were to stop precisely at the point of temperate liberty."

It is difficult to see what led Jefferson to make these remarks unless it be that in periods of national stress even the best minds fail to see clearly. As a matter of fact those who had come *previous* to the founding of "America's Republic", who had fought in the Revolution and had *created* the Republic had all come from monarchial countries. Why those coming after them should be so different is hard to see. The truth of the matter seems to be that the country was suffering from the usual war reaction; an influence which was even more clearly operative in the case of the Alien Law, enacted in 1798, authorizing the President to deport any alien whom he might consider dangerous. But the anti-alien movement soon died down and for about thirty years peace reigned with reference to immigration.

During the fourth decade of the nineteenth century, however, the anti-immigrant movement began to assume new proportion. During those years, the inward flowing stream was beginning to take on something of an incursion as we have seen. Since the greater part of the immigrants were Irish Catholics the anti-Catholic feelings once more came to the surface, especially in those sections (the South particularly) where it had been planted during colonial days. The Native American movement, started in 1835 and for a decade or more directed its efforts against the "Irish Papists." The Know-Nothing party took up the cudgel in the early fifties. To it, most if not all immigrants were paupers and criminals. It demanded stricter naturalization laws, the restriction of the privileges of foreigners in the United States and "America for Americans." Much agitation was carried on, many conventions were held, platforms framed, resolutions drawn up and broadcast through the press, bills were introduced into and investigations made by Congress.

The investigations conducted by the 25th Congress (1838) produced a thoroughly human document in the form of a report, which sounded the alarm with regard to foreign *"paupers, vagrants, and malefactors."* Many of those who are coming, it declared, are "laboring under the infirmities of old age, whose days of usefulness and vigor have been spent in England, or upon the continent of Europe"; many who are "laboring under mental aberration, evidently of long standing, and incurable. Others are idiots, and there is hardly any degree of mental

infirmity which affects mankind, and which is as
various as the shades of human character, inter-
mediate, mere *eccentricity* and absolute frenzy which
may not be found among these, thus cast upon our
country." There are also "convicts from European
states, condemned to imprisonment in their native
country for aggravated offenses against their laws,
and released from imprisonment only on condition
of taking up their residence in this western hemisphere."

A statement which has been repeated times without
number from that day to this then fellows: "At an
early period of our history we possessed an extended
public domain, entirely uncultivated, with numerous
savage tribes skirting our frontier; with a limited
population. . . . The policy of admitting foreigners
. . . was even at that day and under such . . . circumstances doubted by many who were no less distin-
guished for their philanthropy than for their patri-
otism."

No doubt these anti-alien movements were for the
most part political in nature and were intended to
divert public attention from the subject of slavery
which was engrossing the people at the time. However that may be they had no great influence. The
voice of Jefferson and of others had no effect;
the Alien Law of 1798 was repealed in 1801; the
lengthy and alarming Congressional report just
cited failed to excite the public or to provoke Con-

gress to action; the Native American and Know-Nothing movements were comparatively short-lived and died without issue.

IV

As a matter of fact the young nation needed or thought it needed labor forces which were not available at home. The burden of sentiment, therefore, continued to be, in the main, favorable to newcomers. Not only their coming was not restricted but, on the contrary, it was encouraged. The Asylum tradition was still in the building.

Congress passed acts which, indirectly at least, encouraged their coming. The act of 1819 provided for a recording of arriving immigrants and was in the nature of a regulation-of-traffic law. The immigration acts of 1847, 1848 and 1860 were also intended to protect newcomers in the course of their transit across the ocean and therefore served indirectly to encourage immigration.

Official and public opinion was distinctly favorable to the coming of more workers from the Old World. President Tyler, for example, in his message to Congress of June 1, 1841, said: "We hold out to the people of other countries an invitation to come and settle among us as members of our rapidly growing family, and for the blessings which we offer them we require of them to look upon our country as their country and to unite with us in the great

task of preserving our institutions and thereby perpetuating our liberties."

In 1854 Senator Seward declared in Congress:
"The ingress of the foreign population into this
country is a fixed and unchangeable fact. It has
its cause in the condition of society here and in
the condition of society in foreign countries. Nothing could prevent the exodus of the population from
Ireland when they were besieged in their native homes
by famine and pestilence. They came here in obedience to a law which obliged them to come. So it
is of those parts of the population of Germany and
continental Europe which came here. . . . It cannot
remain at home; it must come here, and inasmuch
as it must come here, we are to treat it as if it
were justly and wisely here."

And an unknown writer added: "America pre-
eminently owes its growth and prosperity to the
amalgamation of foreign blood. To cut off, therefore, or to discourage its influx, will be to check
the current from which our very life is drawn. The
better course is evidently to welcome and provide
for this tide of immigration, rather than to oppose
and turn it away; to cherish the good influence it
brings and to regulate the bad, rather than to tram-
ple them both under foot."

The Democratic platform of 1856 even upheld the
doctrine and actually referred to America as the

"Asylum of the oppressed of every nation." During and after the Civil War the shortage of labor was such that the coming of laborers was looked upon with even greater favor. President Lincoln went so far as to advocate the establishment of "A system for the encouragement of immigration." The Republican Party, in its convention of June 7, 1864, approved such a course. In the same year Congress enacted a law bearing the now-incredible title "An Act to Encourage Immigration", which provided greater protection for immigrants during their voyage than previously and established a general assistance office in New York City.

The need for laborers was steadily increasing and that was the dominant consideration. An element of sentiment also kept the country's doors wide open to all comers. There is abundant evidence in the literature of the time that the majority of Americans still regarded America as the refuge of the needy and the home of the religiously and politically oppressed of every nation.

V

In the years immediately after the Civil War, as had been the case after the Revolutionary War, a wave of anti-immigrant sentiment once more arose. In 1866 a singular event occurred and so arrested public attention that it crystallized anti-alien feelings. In Basel, Switzerland, a man committed murder and was convicted. The authorities seemed to have pardoned him on condition that he go to America. What the circumstances of the murder were, what the conditions of the pardon, what became of the convict and whether he actually embarked for and reached America it is difficult to ascertain. The United States consular officer in Switzerland, however, reported the case and it came to the attention of Congress. Congress was disturbed, the public became alarmed. The belief seems to have become general that various European governments were using the United States as a convicts' paradise and as a dumping ground for the riff-raff of Europe. The terrorizing acts of the Molly Maguires in Pennsylvania appeared to lend proof. The matter assumed considerable importance. Congress passed a joint resolution warning the foreign governments "that no such practice shall under any circumstances be repeated." President Andrew Johnson, in the message to Congress of December 3, 1866, referred to it. The "Act to Encourage Immigration" of 1864 was repealed in 1868 by a clause in the consular and diplomatic act, in part, it appears, as a result of agitation following the Basel case. Thus this incident, occurring in a postwar year, directly and indirectly created much anti-immigration sentiment and paved the way for some kind of immigration regulation.

VI

During this period such control of immigration as was exercised by any governmental agency was in the hands of the individual states. Their laws, like those of the Federal government, aimed to protect the immigrant and to safeguard against possible burdens which newcomers might place upon the states. The state laws differed from Federal legislation, however, in that they imposed head taxes upon arriving laborers, bonded ship owners against their bringing persons who might become public charges and provided for the deportation of convicts and paupers. In addition, some states, notably New York and Massachusetts, maintained Commissions, Boards of Immigration, hospitals and detention stations.

With the growth of the power of the Federal Government and the consequent centralization of governmental functions, so characteristic of the period, a controversy arose over the question whether the states had authority to impose taxes and otherwise regulate immigration. This controversy continued for a number of years, culminating in 1875 with a decision of the United States Supreme Court, in which Justice Miller handed down the decision which declared that the regulation of immigration "must of necessity be national in character. It is more than this; for it may properly be called *inter-*

national. It belongs to that class of laws which concern the exterior relation of this whole nation with other nations and governments. . . .

"We are of the opinion that this whole subject has been confided to Congress by the Constitution; that Congress can more appropriately and with more acceptance exercise it than any other body known to our law, state or national; that by providing a system of laws in these matters, applicable to all ports and to all vessels, a serious question, which has long been a matter of contest and complaint, may be effectively and satisfactorily settled."

This decision, then, definitely placed the authority to regulate immigration in the hands of the Federal Government. Congress, however, took no immediate action, and for six years, or down to 1882, chaos reigned. In the meantime, 1,754,826 immigrants entered the country during the years 1876 to 1881, inclusive, and in 1881 a new record was established with more than 669,431 entering. This increased influx, together with the utter absence of control, led to a widespread alarm, and public opinion began to demand regulation.

Two states, New York and California, particularly insisted that Congress should act. New York, unable to impose a head tax on account of the recent Supreme Court decision, was obliged to expend money out of its own coffers to care for the large immigration traffic passing through its principal port. It therefore demanded that Congress should act at once. The New York State Board of Charities brought pressure to bear upon Congress by reiterating the oft-repeated cry that many of the cities and towns in different governments of Europe were sending to this country "blind, crippled, lunatic and other infirm paupers."

In California the first wave of anti-Chinese movement was reaching its height at this time. The Chinese had been welcomed in California during the years after the gold discovery. They were "industrious, tractable, and inoffensive, and were willing to undertake hard, menial, and disagreeable forms of labor—partly work generally done by women— for which native labor was not available under existing conditions." (H. P. Fairchild: *Immigration.*) But of late years they had been subject to bitter and indiscriminate attacks, partly because of the competition they offered to American laborers and partly because of their difference in religion, customs and standards of living. Unable to care for the situation because of national treaties, California insisted that the Federal Government do something about the matter. Congress appointed a special committee on Chinese immigration in 1876, entered into a new treaty with China in 1880 and passed the first Chinese exclusion law in 1882. California's sharp demand led to quick action.

This, however, cared for only one racial group

and one section of the country. The demand still
remained for a general immigration-regulation act.
President Arthur, in his annual message to Congress
of October 12, 1881, recommended the enactment
of such a law.

VII

Thus the way was made clear for a general immigration law. As yet, however, the idea did not prevail that the coming of Old World laborers should
be numerically restricted. The literature of the
period furnishes ample evidence that the public mind
at the time was occupied with questions of head-taxes,
paupers, mental defectives, criminals, rather than
with restriction as such.

In the 47th Congress a general immigration bill
was introduced which dealt precisely with these questions. It was a tiny bill when compared with its
giant successors; were it reproduced it would cover
but one page of this book. It had four brief sections. Section I provided for a tax levy of fifty
cents. Sections II authorized the Secretary of the
Treasury to arrange with the various states for the
detention and care of immigrant convicts, lunatics,
idiots, et cetera. Section III provided for the protection of immigrants against fraud and against loss
upon and after arrival. Section IV enumerated paupers, convicts or accused persons, other than political
offenders, and all persons suffering from any mental
ailment as the excluded classes, and made provision

for their detention and deportation. It is interesting to note that the bill in its original form excluded also dumb, deaf and blind persons but on second thought Congress appears to have taken pity on these and omitted them from the law.

The discussion in the House was as brief as the bill itself. It covers about seven pages of the printed record and it stands in eloquent contrast to the lengthy discussions of recent days. And yet that brief discussion casts interesting light upon the attitude of the time. One Representative fervently defended the bill on the ground that the tax [fifty cents per capita] would "be levied on the steamship companies, not collected of the immigrants."

Representative Dunnel (Minnesota) spoke against the measure. New York reaps the principal fruit of the coming of immigrant laborers, he said, let New York pay the bill. "No city in the Union reaps so rich an income from immigration as the city of New York. It is impossible for the most insignificant immigrant to land in New York and get out of it without leaving one, two, three, four, or five dollars. . . . I am radically opposed to imposing the charge of one dollar, or even fifty cents, upon any man, woman, or child who may land in the city of New York from any portion of the globe."

The act, made law by executive approval on August 3, 1882, was of no great importance in itself, since it dealt primarily with head taxes and with the detention and deportation of undesirable defectives, et cetera. The measure was significant, however, not only because it was the first Federal Immigration Law, but because it introduced the negative principle of *selection-by-rejection* and thereby established a tradition which prevailed in all immigration legislation from that day to 1924. It provided for the *rejection* of certain classes at the lowest rung of the social ladder rather than for the *selection* of the most skilled and fit in capacity or occupation for meeting the economic or social needs of the country.

It is illuminating to note that suggestions for the positive selection of immigrants and for their examination abroad had been made even before this. But Congress would have none of them. That body, like all legislative bodies—usually a drag upon constructive public opinion—could not see the need or the advantage of adopting positive methods. In fact it took Congress more than half a century from the time the suggestion was first made before it saw fit to adopt the visa system (in the 1924 law), and then Congressmen pointed with pride to the accomplishment, as if it were their own creation. Much difficulty and internation illwill might have been prevented had a positive-selective principle been adopted in those early days.

VIII

The time was not ripe for a restriction of immigration, not even for regulation. Laborers the country needed, or thought it needed. And in search of them its citizens ransacked the earth. Numberless letters, maps, guides, views, reminiscences, pocket geographies, diaries, pocket companions, journals, histories and even novels presenting the opportunities of the New World made their way to the Old World. These presented the most minute information, offered all kinds of advice, told of the laws governing the settlement of land, the kind of food a traveler should eat on the way. Private land companies and railroads advertised widely. Most western states appropriated large sums of money to establish information agencies in Europe.

In answer to these calls, Old World laborers poured into the country in ever increasing numbers: 2,350,000 between 1861 and 1870; nearly 3,000,000 in the following decade; 5,250,000 from 1881 to 1890, with a new high mark of 788,992 in 1882. They scattered into every part of the Union wherever their labor was needed. In 1850 nine out of every ten foreign born were residing in the northern and central states—six in the North Atlantic, three in the North Central division; one in every ten resided in the southern and western states. But as the West opened up the proportional number of them steadily decreased in the North Atlantic, the South Atlantic and the South Central divisions; while in the North Central and the Western divisions, the land of opportunity *par excellence* in those days, their number

steadily increased. In the ten-year period from 1880
to 1890 they turned more to the Atlantic belt, for
reasons we shall presently indicate.

They came mainly from the British Isles, Germany and the Scandinavian countries, with comparatively few from France, Switzerland and Canada.
The Germans established principally in the North
Central states where agriculture drew them.   In
1850 over half of their entire number—more than
a million—lived in these states.   Between 1870 and
1880 sixty-two out of every hundred Germans reaching this country went there to reside.   Their greatest
single group, one-sixth of their whole number, lived
in New York State in 1890.

The Irish clung to the North Atlantic division,
where, in 1860, two-thirds of them lived.   As in the
case of the Germans, their greatest single center was
in New York State.   Many Irishmen, however, were
caught in the westward movement; large groups of
them entered the coal fields, especially the anthracite
regions of Pennsylvania.   Fifty thousand were scattered through Indiana, Illinois and Michigan in
1850.   The Irish went largely into mining and the
manufacturing industries.

The Scandinavians made their way into Minnesota,
Wisconsin, the Dakotas.   The British, who at the
time of the 1860 Census numbered 487,775, were
scattered all over the country, some in the South,
many were in Wisconsin and other northwestern

states. As with the Germans, about one-fourth of them stayed in New York. The opportunities for farming and the mineral wealth in the southwestern part of Wisconsin lured many of them to that state. In 1880 the Scotch still continued to go to the North Atlantic States in larger numbers than to the North Central States; the Welsh went for the most part to the North Central States. Nearly one-half of the increase which took place in the Western division was made up of English people.

A round century of national life passed and immigrants still kept pouring into the country practically unhindered. America not only permitted them to enter freely, but *encouraged* them to come. Americans protected the migrants during the voyage, welcomed them on arrival, took care of those who needed it after reaching this country, gave most of those who came a chance to work. The rapidly expanding country needed, or thought it needed laborers; it might have theorized about the advisability of producing population of its own to supply that need, but the fact is it did not.

The laborers of Europe, on the other hand, needed the opportunity which America gave them, and needed it badly. They too might have philosophized that it was better for them to remain in their own countries and effect social reforms, but that was not the course they followed. The New World oppor-

tunity was too great, immediate, tangible. They
followed.

It was this combination of forces that gave rise to
the tradition that America was the land of opportunity. Nor was it merely a tradition. It was perhaps the greatest single reality in the life of the
laborer of the Old World, and one of the most
genuine forces operating in the life of the United
States. Those who were able to come certainly realized, some more, some less, the glorious meaning of
that tradition and reality. And only those who find
themselves imprisoned in circumstances not of their
own making, who dream of America and still have
been or may be prohibited in the future from entering the Promised Land, only they can possibly com-
prehend the awful meaning of the passing of the
Asylum tradition. This is no argument against
restriction, but only a record of facts. Tradition
and its reality are no more. An avalanche of changes
has descended upon us, changes in objective fact and
in outlook, and to an examination of these the reader
is now invited.

CHAPTER III

THE PASSING OF THE TRADITION

Wide open and unguarded stand our gates, . . .
And through them presses a wild a motley throng—

   ·   ·   ·   ·   ·   ·   ·

Flying the Old World's poverty and scorn;
These bringing with them unknown gods and rites,
Those, tiger passions, here to stretch their claws.
In streets and alley what strange tongues are these;
Accents of menace alien to our air,
Voices that once the Tower of Babel knew!
O Liberty, white Goddess! is it well
To leave the gates unguarded? . . .
                —*Thomas Bailey Aldrich,* 1892.

I

Down to about 1880, therefore, the Asylum tradition remained practically intact. Beginning with that time, however, the attitude of the United States toward Old World laborers experienced a decided and more or less permanent change. The question naturally arises; had the ideals of the American people changed or had objective conditions so altered as to make this departure from the traditional attitude a necessity?

The key answer, no doubt, is found in the economic history of the United States. Prior to this time this country was primarily an agricultural nation, its people engaged chiefly in tilling the soil or extracting the natural resources; foreign commerce depended almost entirely upon the agricultural and extractive industries. After 1880, however, the manufacturing industries experienced a most extraordinary expansion, a fact to which we shall refer more at length later.

As this development took place Old World laborers began to pour in in unprecedented numbers, reaching a new high mark in 1882, when 788,992 immigrants entered the country. Much has been said as to whether these came because of the industrial expansion or whether their coming caused the new industrial activity. The Immigration Commission pointed out, years afterwards, that no conclusive answer can be given to this question. "Whether this great immigration movement was caused by the industrial development or whether the fact that a practically unlimited and available supply of cheap labor existed in Europe was taken advantage of for the purpose of expanding the industries, cannot well be demonstrated." It seems reasonable to conclude, however, that the coming of Old World laborers materially hastened industrial expansion, not only by supplying large volumes of unskilled labor, but also by furnishing considerable numbers of skilled persons. Moreover, as remarks H. C. Emery in *Cambridge Modern History* (Vol. 7),

"Americans, attributing too much to the native character, are frequently inclined to forget that many
of the most striking cases of success in the industrial
and commercial world have been those of poor
immigrants."

II

Those who arrived after 1880, however, came
in the main from an entirely different group of
nations from those who had come before. Previous
to 1880, as we have seen, the majority of immigrants
came from northwestern Europe: from Great Britain,
Germany, and the Scandinavian countries. With
1882 large streams began to come from southern and
southeastern Europe, particularly from Italy,
Austria-Hungary and Russia.

This shifting of immigration sources was due to
three principal causes. First, the very increase in
the manufacturing activities we have just mentioned.
To supply the labor needs of this expansion new
sources had to be tapped, for obvious reasons. Those
who had come here previous to 1880 had, as we
have seen, gone primarily into agriculture or were
already fixed in such industrial establishments as
had developed before that time. Consequently it
was difficult, if not impossible, for the new industrial
interests to get workers from that source. Moreover, those of the older "races" who were coming
tended to join relatives and friends and thus to drift

into the same occupations and localities. In the
next place, the labor situation in the northwestern
European nations was changing greatly. Those
countries were themselves experiencing great industrial expansion, which called for the conservation of
their labor forces; and governments, notably that of
Germany, began to look unfavorably upon emigration; they enacted laws prohibiting the solicitation
of labor by outsiders and aimed in other ways to
prevent the exodus of their laborers. Those nations
also were taking great strides in labor organization,
advance of wages, conditions of labor, and in supplying disability and accident insurance. These improvements, so notable in western Europe at the
time, largely removed the inducements to migrate,
by making general conditions at home nearly equivalent to those prevailing in America.

The change in the sources of imported labor was
due also to the fact that employers in America seem
to have *preferred* laborers from new quarters. The
organized labor movement was making rapid growth
at the time, the recruits coming from American
or western European workers already in this country. Employers, therefore, preferred workers from
countries other than those which had supplied them
in former years, since it was precisely the latter
who, together with Americans, were "joining the
union" and causing [*sic*] industrial unrest. Moreover, as remarks Max Farrand, "a variety of races

. . . made organization of workmen more difficult where many languages and dialects were spoken, a union on a common basis was long impossible; and employers were unquestionably following such a policy deliberately."

American capital, therefore, set out to discover new sources of labor and to that purpose ransacked the very ends of the earth. Steamship lines for the first time plowed deep into the Mediterranean, agents went abroad, offered various inducements, brought in foreign laborers as strike breakers and under contract for specific periods. E. A. Ross records (*The Century Magazine, Vol. 87*) that the Slavs and Magyars were introduced into Pennsylvania by mine operators looking for more tractable miners. Two shiploads of strike breakers, Hungarians in this case, were brought into Drifton as early as 1870. In 1904 during a strike in the coal field near Birmingham, Alabama, many southern Europeans were brought in, and during the 1907 strike in the iron mines of northern Minnesota one company imported large numbers of Montenegrins and other southeastern Europeans as strike breakers. And in the wake of imported laborers came many, of course, of their own accord.

III

It was inevitable that conflict should arise between the laborers already here, whether native or foreign born, and the new immigrants. The latter not only were different, spoke strange tongues, wore strange dress, ate strange food, lived in strange ways, worshiped strange gods; but also were submissive, accepted lower wages, forced Americans out of employment, or to lower their standards of living.

A clash followed, partly economic, partly social, in part based upon objective fact and in part upon the figment of imagination. But it was dynamically real. American laborers were infuriated. The Knights of Labor conducted vigorous propaganda, won the support of the press and of Congress and brought about the passage of the 1885 immigration law, by which entrance of laborers under contract was prohibited. This was the first tangible blow to be dealt to the open door tradition and practice. The law of self-preservation was at work on both sides, and those who possessed the vantage ground won the day.

The industrial disturbances of the period, due in part to this very clash and also to the irascible temper of too-rapidly expanding industries, contributed their share to the breaking up of the Asylum tradition. These disturbances were many and severe: the industrial depression of 1882, the so-called "Grant and Ward" panic of 1884-86 and the prolonged railway strike of 1885. Particularly violent was the Chicago Riot of May, 1886, in which

a German and an English anarchist were the principal leaders and "anarchists, laborers and mechanics, mostly Germans" the main participants.   A
German anarchist threw a bomb, resulting in casualties, eight anarchists were indicted, one German and
one Englishman were condemned to life imprisonment, three Germans were condemned to die and
were hanged on November 11, 1887.   "All thoughtful citizens," says Rhodes in *History of the United
States*, "must have been interested to note that six
out of the eight who stood trial were Germans, as
was also the thrower of the bomb.   This fellow had
lived in this country not more than two years and
could not speak English. . . ."

In the next decade occurred the Homestead strike
of 1892 in which a Russian anarchist attempted the
assassination of Henry Clay Frick, chairman of the
Carnegie Steel Company; the panic of 1893, the
American Railway Union Strike of 1894, the arrest
of Debs in 1894, and the Henry George single-tax
movement, whose principles were considered *very*
radical.

IV

Two other sets of conditions also contributed to
the breaking up of the tradition: the concentration
of foreign born laborers in the industrial zone and
the depletion of free lands.   In the 1880-90 decade
the foreign born in the United States increased by

2,570,000. Of these about 2,216,000 were in the North Atlantic and North Central States in 1890, and of the 9,250,000 foreign born in the United States in that year 7,948,000 were located in these two divisions.

This herding of new immigrants alarmed the public. Books descriptive of immigrant communities came into vogue. The first was Jacob Riis's now famous work, *How the Other Half Lives* (1890). Although evidently intended to awaken the interest of the American public in the conditions of immigrants, this book so vividly described the "slum" and the conditions under which Old World laborers lived in the New, that it actually produced the opposite effect. The book was read widely and may even now be seen in many American homes, in its original edition.

The influence that book had upon the American mind must have been great. Henry Cabot Lodge, who, as we shall see, became a prominent advocate of immigration restriction, and whose opposition to southern and southeastern Europeans came out more clearly later, made very shrewd use of Riis's story. Specifically mentioning the book, Mr. Lodge said, in *The North American Review* of January 1891: "The condition of a large mass of the laboring population in the city of New York is enough to alarm every thinking man; and this dreadful condition of things is intensified every day by the steady inflow of immigration, which is constantly pulling down the wages of the working people of New York and affecting in a similar way the entire labor market of the United States."

The depletion of public lands also made a profound impression upon the American mind and naturally was connected with immigration. The argument was repeatedly advanced that the exhaustion of the public domain had removed one of the best openings for the foreigner without capital and since the resources of the West and South were being rapidly developed, the opportunities for the great mass of unskilled laborers had disappeared. General Francis A. Walker, who had been Director of the Census, kept reiterating this fact all through this period, calling attention to "the complete exhaustion of free public lands of the United States." To top this movement there came, in 1890, the momentous announcement of the United States Bureau of Census that the frontier had come to an end.

V

The cumulative effect of these events: the greatly enlarged stream of immigration, the industrial depression, the labor disturbances, the concentration of immigrants in industrial centers, the detailed descriptions of immigrant communities, the exhaustion of the public domain—coming as they did all in the single decade 1880-90, made a deep impression, and seem to have stirred the American public.

Feelings against "foreigners" became so intense during the latter part of the 1880-90 decade that the press of the time seems to have sounded the very depths of the dictionary for every possible opprobrious epithet known to the English language. The Bohemians, Chinese, Germans, Gypsies, Hungarians, "Huns", Italians, "Oriental Jews", Poles and Czechs, "Latin-and-Slavic-element", and Russo-Poles", received special mention.

The vituperation poured upon these "races" or "nationalities", as they were called, was expressed in every conceivable term. Here are a few of these choice epithets applied to immigrants in *one single year*.[1] Immigrants were called barbarians or polygamous relics of barbarism, half savages; human dregs of all the earth, diseased elements, the off-scouring of Europe and Asia, human and inhuman rubbish, heterogeneous hordes, a motley herd, scum and riff-raff; paupers, filthy mendicants, or pauper populations of the Old World; lazy loafers, vagabonds, ignorant, charlatans, lazzaroni, prodioseros; adventurers, seekers of fortune, worthless; mis-

---

[1] All but a few of these expressions are taken from the literature of a single year, 1887, the year when ten of the participants of the Chicago riot were condemned and hung. cf. *Public Opinion*, Vol. III (1887), index under "Immigrants and Immigration"; *Forum*, Vol. III (1887), pp. 533, 537, 542; *Nation*, Vol. XLV. (1887), pp. 518, 519.

creants, engenders of denominationalism and sec-
tarianism; enfeebled persons, diseased persons, weak,
vile and hungry outcasts from hospitals, prisons and
poor houses, landed here not only to stay themselves,
but to transmit hereditary taints to the third and
fourth generations;[1] ignorant, insane, irredeemable
maniacs; thieves and thugs, jail-birds, lawless loafers
. . . whose highest ambition is to have the freedom
to steal the fruits of the labors of others; lawless,
immoral, wicked, vicious, criminal; social dregs and
rogues; vicious off-scouring of old political societies;
cranks and malcontents; undutiful and unpatriotic,
social pests and incendiaries; inciters to pillage and
assassination; agitators . . . that anathematize our
laws and institutions; foreign mischief makers; rant-
ing apostles of disorder; turbulent foreign proletariat; enemies of the state, whose hospitality they
have sought unbidden.

The immigrant was now "investigated" and
"studied" from boyhood to the grave. His effects
upon politics and citizenship, his insanity and
illiteracy, criminal tendency and pauperism, blindness and deafness, feeblemindedness, occupation and
destination all were now looked into. And everywhere, in everything the immigrant laborer was
found wanting—"a menace."

[1] *Forum,* December, 1889.

One of the worst attacks ever made upon the immigrant laborer was that by Hjalmar H. Boyesen, appearing in the *Forum* of July, 1887. According to this writer the fourteen millions of immigrants who had come to the United States since the founding of the Republic had immensely complicated the problem of self-government, by their alienism in thought and conduct, subjecting the Constitution to the severest strain, not absorbing into the native population, becoming disturbing elements, an unexpended surplus in the labor market, creating discontent and disorder. He attacked the Germans especially for maintaining their own churches, clubs and associations, and for showing a sense of "national superiority to the people whose hospitality they are enjoying . . . They aspire to Germanize, in part, the country of their adoption." These newcomers as a whole, according to this author, were responsible for the "terrible doings of the Knights of Labor. . . . Every steamship unloading upon our shores its motley herd of Germans, Bohemians, Hungarians, Poles and Italians, reënforces the ranks of this party of destruction and prepares the way for a new revolution, or attempt at revolution." Sooner or later they all find their places among the subverters of the social order . . . for "all the lower strata of society, and particularly the immigrated portion of it, are, at present, hungry, not necessarily for food, but for all the good things of life which are beyond their reach."

VI

State and Federal investigations, reports, recommendations fell pell-mell one upon another and vied with pronouncements of political parties in condemning immigrants. In 1886 the Wisconsin Bureau of Labor Statistics made an investigation and found among the employers of that state an "unanimity in favor of restricting immigration" and "an unexpected sentiment in favor of cutting off immigration of all kinds forever, or for periods varying in length from two to twenty years," a sentiment "heartily and earnestly supported by the larger portion of Wisconsin's Scandinavian and German citizens." The report was quoted widely. United States Commissioner of Labor Carrol D. Wright, in the same year, declared that the "doctrine that the United States offers an asylum to the world" was a "somewhat dangerous" one, or at least "a doctrine now largely out of place."

In Congress the matter came to the fore. Standing committees on immigration were created and bills were introduced in nearly every session. In 1888 a congressional committee found that "the laws prohibiting the importation of contract laborers, convicts and paupers were being extensively evaded owing to the lack of machinery to enforce them" and that the country demanded a stricter enforcement of existing laws. In 1889 a standing committee of the House and Senate was created. The Ford Com-

mittee made an "investigation" of the testimony and
opinion recording kind and published a voluminous
report consisting of some eight hundred pages
besides one hundred and fifty-seven pages of "reports
of diplomatic and consular officers concerning emigration from Europe to the United States."

A report to the House in the Fiftieth Congress
declared that immigration had been *in the past* an
important factor in the growth and development of
the Republic. Those who came to America in the
early years, were largely composed of honest, industrious people in sympathy with our form of government, proving a most desirable addition to our population, harmonizing with it and ripening into law
abiding and worthy citizens.

"But can this be said of a large portion of the
immigrants we are now receiving? The Committee
believe not." Among the newcomers are many
anarchists, coming from Germany through England.
"They have proven a lawless, turbulent class, and
the whole country is familiar with their recent acts
of violence. . . ." Many are of a very low order
of intelligence who are duped into immigrating by
steamship companies and contractors in this country and "come here with no intention of becoming
citizens."

VII

Here and there someone dared to speak in behalf
of the immigrants. Thus the editor of the *Milwau-*

kee Sentinel wrote in 1889, "In the talk in favor
of restricting immigration of the wrong kind, we
are in danger of forgetting that we still want immigration of the right kind. The coming of scamps
and paupers is no reason why we should abandon
the idea of making America the home of all who are
fit to come if they choose to become American citizens
—we need to require that those who come shall give
evidence of their purpose and fitness to qualify themselves for intelligent citizenship. Beyond that, there
should be no restriction if America is to work out
her grand destiny."

Professor Mayo-Smith of Columbia, although
recognizing the social problems immigration creates,
wrote, in 1890, "In seeking a remedy for the present
abuses there is constant danger that we may be
simply groping back to medieval restrictions and
vexations which are incompatible with the conditions
of modern life. There is danger also that a spirit
of chauvinism, or of petty trade jealousy, or of
demagogy may take possession of the movement,
and exploit it for its own contemptible purposes.
The control of immigration must be free from the
base cry of 'America for the Americans,' and from
the narrow spirit of trade-unionism, or of a selfish
desire to monopolize the labor market. It must find
its justification in the needs of the community, and
in the necessity of selecting those elements which
will contribute to the harmonious development of
our civilization."

Eugene Schuyler, who had lived in Italy for a number of years, and had studied Italian immigration, came to the defense of the Italian: "Taking everything together, it would seem that the Italians, in spite of poverty and illiteracy, are . . . a desirable element to fuse with our motley population. They bring to us the logical qualities of the Latin race, and they show in the long run the effect of an experience which no other people in Europe has had —of over two thousand years of civilization."

Here and there some other writer added that immigrants *could* be naturalized if the public took an interest in them, that their coming was a benefit in that they increased consumption, that many brought substantial sums varying from $500 to $2,000, that there was still room for newcomers, especially in the South, and a congressional committee of the 51st Congress even came to the point of almost saying a good word for the "new" immigrant.[1]

It was too late, however. The Old World laborer had done his work; he was no longer needed now. The "asylum for all the world" tradition was no more. That tradition, which at the beginning of the 1880-90 decade had been accepted as a fact, had

[1] House Report 3472, 51st Congress, 2nd Session (Jan., 1891.)

now been questioned, challenged, attacked, placed on the defensive, and had lost its hold as a dominant force in the life of America; it had gone to return no more as a great and noble national idea.   And the stage was set for a new act in the drama of human migrations.

CHAPTER IV

We've dug your million ditches,
  We've built your endless roads,
We've fetched your wood and water,
  And bent beneath your loads,
We've done the lowly labor,
  Despised by your own breed——
And now you won't admit us
  Because we cannot read.
                    —*Author Unknown.*

I

THE Asylum tradition having for all practical purposes been broken, it now remained to devise and adopt means to make effective the new attitude. This was not an easy task, however, since the country was in the midst of its industrial expansion, and a sudden cutting off of immigrant labor would be unwise, if not impossible.

Late in the eighties two methods came to be advocated for restricting immigration: consular certification of immigrants abroad, and the Literacy Test. The former, by far the more constructive of the two, was set aside, to be resurrected, as we shall see, nearly forty years later. The Literacy Test, on the other hand, seized and for a quarter of a century held the imagination of those who would restrict immigration. This was due to the belief, undoubtedly partly based on fact, that large numbers of immigrants then coming to the United States were illiterates. Actually no one knew what the situation was; and even the Congressional Joint Committee's investigation of 1890-91 was unable to produce any real evidence. Nevertheless, the belief became increasingly current that large numbers of laborers then coming from southeastern Europe were illiterate, and that if a Literacy Test were adopted, immigration would be considerably reduced.

II

The story of the Literacy Test: its background, birth and sturdy growth, the repeated onsets it made, and the repulses it experienced both in and out of congressional halls, and of its final adoption and practically fruitless victory—altogether constitutes one of the most interesting and dramatic acts in legislation history. It is also most illuminating in that it shows how large a part partisanship or personal predeliction may play in legislation.

The Test was born in Massachusetts, which in colonial days, as we have seen, was one of the most persistent adherents to exclusiveness. Edward W. Bemis presented it to the public through the pages of the *Andover Review* of March, 1888, as the most practical and simple mode of restriction. "This may be, for aught I know," he wrote, "the first public advocacy of it. But it has commended itself wherever I have presented it in conversation and lecture in many states of the East and West, and by leaders of trades unions as well as by all other classes with scarcely a dissenting voice. It is this: Admit no single person over sixteen, and no man over that age who cannot read and write in his own language."

Massachusetts also furnished the most ardent advocates of the Test. Henry Cabot Lodge became a sort of godfather to it from the first and throughout its history stood behind it like an ever present paternal influence. In fact, the suggestion has been heard that Mr. Lodge, worshiper of formal education that he was, was the real originator of the Test. The first organized support of it also came out of the same state in the form of the Immigration Restriction League, established in Boston in 1894, a body which proved an ever present help throughout the proposal's long and tempestuous life. And it was Massachusetts' Senator who first carried it into the congressional halls in the form of a bill introduced on March 18, 1896.

III

In the Senate Mr. Lodge was the principal advocate of the measure; in fact from the Congressional

Record it appears that only two other senators seem to have been sufficiently concerned either to support or oppose it. The Senator from Massachusetts, however, presented a comprehensive and convincing argument. The Literacy Test, he argued, would reduce the number of immigrants admitted, and what was more, it would cut down those coming from southeastern Europe who, in recent years, had contributed most largely to immigration. The bill did not again come up for discussion until May 14, and passed on December 17, 1896, with a 52 to 10 vote.

Representative McCall, also of Massachusetts, introduced a similar bill into the House and presented arguments along the same line as those of Senator Lodge. Here also the opposition was meager and the bill passed on May 20, 1896 by a vote of 195 to 26.

But President Cleveland, who, it needs to be kept in mind, was a Democrat, while Senator Lodge was a Republican, refused to affix his executive signature to this act of Congress, and returned it with his veto on March 2, 1897.

The bill, he wrote in his veto message, represents "a radical departure from our national policy relating to immigration. Heretofore we have welcomed all who came to us from other lands except those whose moral or physical condition or history threatened danger to our national welfare and safety. . . . A century's stupendous growth, largely due to the

assimilation and thrift of millions of sturdy and
patriotic adopted citizens, attests the success of this
generous and free-handed policy. . . . It is not
claimed . . . that an excess of population over-
crowds our land. [Moreover], ability to read and
write . . . affords a misleading test of contented
industry and supplies unsatisfactory evidence of
desirable citizenship or a proper apprehension of the
benefits of our institutions."

Thus the Literacy Test suffered its first blow.
But behind it stood the figure of the tenacious little
man who was destined to remain in Congress many
years after President Cleveland had gone out of
office and out of life. It would surely reappear on
the floors of the Capitol, and reappear it did.

IV

Meanwhile, the United States was moving toward
industrial supremacy. "The discovery and utilization of material resources on an unprecedented scale,
the extension of the domestic market by the settlement of the West, the improvement and the cheapen-
ing of transportation facilities and the more complete application of labor-saving devices—" all
occurring for the most part in the two decades 1880-
1900 gave new impetus to the nation's industrial
activity. (Bogart: *Economic History of the United
States.*)

In manufacturing alone the country was making

gigantic strides, by 1894 attaining first rank, a place it has held ever since. Later, during the 1899-1919 period, the manufacturing industries increased 40 per cent in the number of establishments and experienced a large expansion in the size of the plants, 80 per cent in the number of laborers employed, 400 per cent in the total capital invested, and 460 per cent in the value of the products.

Nature and national events had conspired in locating most of this manufacturing activity north of the Potomac and Ohio and east of the Mississippi rivers, and especially in southern New England, in New York, New Jersey and Pennsylvania. The States of New York, Pennsylvania, Illinois, Massachusetts and Ohio, though containing but one-third of the population of the United States in 1910, in 1909 had 51 per cent of the total number of wage earners in manufacturing industries, over 52 per cent of the value added by manufacture. New York City alone was producing in value nearly one-tenth of the country's manufactured products.

It was natural that the workers who were coming to this country at the time should go principally into the industrial zone. It was there that their labor was wanted. So they went in increasing proportions into the manufacturing states. In 1890 46 per cent of all foreign born in the United States were located in the North Atlantic states and 40.6 per cent in the North Central states; in 1910 over

one-third were residing in the former states and
nearly one-half in the latter. By 1920, whereas the
foreign born whites made up only 13 per cent of the
total population, they constituted nearly one-sixth
of the population of the East North Central States,
over one-fifth that of the Middle Atlantic States, and
over one-fourth of that of the New England States.
During the 1900-1920 period the North Atlantic
division alone increased by over 2,083,000 foreign
born, or 56.6 per cent of the total increase for this
class in the entire country.

Immigrants not only concentrated in the predominantly industrial divisions, but they congregated
even more in the principal industrial states within
those divisions. In 1900 not only 46 per cent of all
foreign born in the country were in the North Atlantic division, but also 36 per cent or over one-third of
all the foreign born in that division were centered
in the three states of Massachusetts, New York and
Pennsylvania and 18 per cent or nearly one-fifth in
the single state of New York. In 1920 the North
Atlantic division had a little over 42 per cent of the
country's foreign born; Massachusetts, New York
and Pennsylvania alone contained 38 per cent; the
single state of New York 20 per cent. Of all the
foreign born whites in the United States in 1920, over
one-third (35.8 per cent) were living in New York,
New Jersey and Pennsylvania; nearly one-fourth
(23.5 per cent) in Ohio, Indiana, Illinois, Michigan

and Wisconsin—thus about three-fifths of all the foreign born whites in the United States were located in the eight leading manufacturing states.

In Rhode Island 28.7 per cent of the total population were foreign born, in Massachusetts, 28.0 per cent, Connecticut, 27.3 per cent, New York, 26.8 per cent, New Jersey, 23.4 per cent, New Hampshire, 20.6 per cent, Minnesota, 20.4 per cent, North Dakota, 20.3 per cent, Michigan, 19.8 per cent, Illinois, 18.6 per cent, Wisconsin, 17.5 per cent.

V

As this concentration of foreign born workers took place the fear became prevalent that the immigrants were displacing the native stock and were tearing apart the fabric of America's life. Consequently, more investigations, more reports were made, more articles written, more speeches delivered, more descriptions of immigrant communities appeared.

When in 1907 the greatest annual stream of foreign born laborers that ever made its way to the United States (1,285,349) was entering the country, the Literacy Test proposal was resurrected once more and the battle for its passage became fiercer than ever before. In Congress the protagonists of restriction still believed that the Literacy Test offered a panacea for all the immigration ills. And so they pushed for its passage.

By a joker in the bill then before Congress, however, the Test was sidetracked and in its stead a clause introduced authorizing the President to appoint a commission to investigate and make a report to Congress on the whole subject of immigration, with particular reference to the best methods to secure restrictions. The Immigration Commission was appointed and "investigated" in this country and in many other countries for three years, spending $900,000. And when at the end of its investigation the Commission brought back its report, consisting of forty-seven volumes, lo and behold! among the millions of words contained in the report, there were two significant phrases: "the reading and writing test" . . . "the most feasible single method" of restricting immigration.

So again appeared the Literacy Test, more vigorous than ever before. During Taft's administration once more it passed both Houses of Congress and for the second time in its career it journeyed to the White House, only to be sent back again with the President's veto. The veto message which, on February 14, 1913, accompanied the Test back to the Capitol Hill, was as brief and mild as Cleveland's had been long and vigorous. It simply referred to Secretary of Labor Nagel's letter which declared the Act embodying the Test discriminatory and almost impossible to administer.

By this time the Literacy Test had gone through

sixteen years or more of warfare, of attempt after
attempt to find a niche in the law of the land, of
heated debates in Congress, numerous discussions
in the rostra of the country, numberless magazine
articles. Everybody seemed to see the salvation of
America in it. Its supporters were among the most
influential men in the country. And yet whenever it
reached the very verge of triumph, back it would
fall to ignominious defeat.

VI

The Literacy Test might never have become law
had not the World War come to play its important
rôle in the story of man. During the year immediately following President Taft's veto large numbers
of laborers rushed out of Europe and into America
as if driven by a prevision of the impending doom
that was soon to overtake humanity. Nearly one
million and a quarter immigrants entered the United
States in 1913-14; and soon after the close of the
fiscal year the European conflagration broke out.

As Europe became involved in strife the number
of incoming immigrants diminished greatly, dropping
to 326,700 in 1914-15 (the lowest mark since 1889)
while 204,074 persons of foreign birth left the United
States for Europe, chiefly to join the colors of their
native countries. The fight for restriction instead
of waning took on renewed vigor. While Europe
was engaged in mortal combat it was an opportune

time to push the battle to a finish. Arriving immigrants were comparatively few; those who were here,
deprived of their leaders, many of whom had gone
to fight for their native countries, could have no
great political weight. Europe itself, too deeply
engrossed in a life and death struggle, could pay no
attention or even notice what America would do in
the matter of immigration, while the State Department was otherwise too busy to interfere.

Had constructive thought prevailed, advantage
might have been taken of the situation and a worth-
while method sought for solving the thorny immigration problem. But no! The restrictionist's eye
was fixed on the Literacy Test. The Test was
pushed to the front again, with redoubled vigor
and renewed purpose; and in the latter part of 1914
a bill embodying it again passed both Houses of Congress. But when it reached the White House it was
sent back, on January 28, 1915, with the word
"VETO" written upon it.

In his veto message, President Wilson wrote:
"This bill embodies a radical departure from the
tradition and long-established policy of this country, a policy in which our people have conceived the
very character of their government to be expressed,
the very mission and spirit of the nation in respect
to its relation to the peoples of the world outside
their borders. It seeks to all but close entirely the
gates of asylum which have always been open to

those who could find nowhere else the right and
opportunity of constitutional agitation for what
they conceived to be the natural and inalienable
rights of men; and it excludes those to whom the
opportunities of elementary education have been
denied, without regard to their character, their purpose, or their natural capacity." Led by Senator
Lodge, Congress attempted to pass the measure over
the President's veto, but failed.

Statistics on immigrant illiteracy had been made
available by this time. Out of 11,726,606 immigrants, fourteen years of age and over, who had
been admitted to the United States during the 1900-
14 period, 3,116,182, or over one-fourth (26.5 per
cent) could neither read nor write. These facts gave
restrictionists added conviction that the Literacy
Test *was* the *summum bonum*. With greater determination they set to the task of forcing its passage.
So in 1916 the Test once more made its appearance
in Congress. It passed the House on March 10,
1916, and the Senate on December 14. It made its
way to the White House, only to drag itself toward
Capitol Hill on January 29, 1917 with President
Wilson's second veto, and the fourth veto it had
received.

VII

Congress, already at odds with the Chief Executive, was prepared for the blow. Two days after the

return of the act accompanied by President Wilson's second veto, the House Immigration Committee placed a printed report in the hands of the Representatives, in which it urged passing the bill over the President's veto. It was a last bitter fight for the Test.

The report employed the usual arguments, applied from almost the very beginning of national life to all immigrants: "Foreign countries look with favor upon emigration to America of diseased and defective persons; the number of insane has been increasing with the increase in arrival of peoples from southern and southeastern Europe; this section also adds vagrants and those who are afflicted with tuberculosis. [Moreover there is] an oversupply of unskilled labor in the industries of the country as a whole."

The burden of the report was: The Literacy Test *must* pass! This measure has come up in almost every Congress for the last fifteen or twenty years, has received the approval of the Immigration Commission as the most feasible single method of restricting undesirable immigrants; it has the support of Mr. Gompers and the labor and farmer organizations of the country; many of the large patriotic organizations have for years, by action of their national and local conventions indorsed this test and petitioned Congress to enact it into law. The legislatures of Ohio, Virginia, Tennessee, Vermont, and of many other states passed resolutions and petitioned Congress to pass it. Within the last week, continued the report, the Women's Republican Club of the City of New York had, by resolution, asked Congress to pass it, and the great majority of them indorse it. Then why not pass it?

What *if* the Test is not a true measure of "quality or of character or personal fitness?" It *is* "the most feasible method" of keeping out undesirable immigrants, for reducing numbers, for keeping out at least 200,000 immigrants from the United States in any normal year. On February 1, 1917, after extended debate, the House passed the bill over the President's veto, by a vote of 287 to 106, and four days later the Senate did likewise by a vote of 62 to 19, and the measure became law on February 5, 1917.

Thus the Literary Test goes down into immigration and American history with an extraordinary and most unique record; introduced at least as early as 1888 and dragging on for almost thirty years, it was favored of politicians, race-purists, economists, political scientists, and newspaper men; voted upon and actually passed in one chamber or the other of Congress thirty-two times; it had had an average of 216 to 79 votes in the 14 recorded votes in the House and of 53 to 15 in the 10 recorded votes in the Senate; advocated by various congressional committees and by the Immigration Commission;

written upon and discussed without end; disapproved
by three Presidents, vetoed four times, failing to pass
over executive veto thrice; it finally became law
without the signature of the President—a remarkable record, indeed, the equal of which the annals of
American history can scarcely show.

VIII

When the law of February 5, 1917 is closely
examined it is found to have made no fundamental
improvements.   It did make certain important
changes: it codified all previous immigration legislation, extended the list of those subject to exclusion, including among these the peoples of the
so-called "Barred Zone" which the law created;
imposed greater fines upon steamship companies for
bringing people subject to exclusion; and strength-
ened the provisions concerning deportation.   In
exempting children under sixteen, accompanying
either parent, from the head tax, the law introduced
a constructive element in that it encouraged the
coming of families as against individuals.   The law,
like that of 1907, recognized the necessity of dealing
with the immigration problem internationally when
it authorized the President to call, or appoint representatives to participate in, international conferences
on immigration.

But the *literacy provision* which was the main
feature of the law, and over which such a relentless

fight had been waged for more than a quarter of a century, did nothing else than merely add *illiterates* to the list of excluded classes. This provision, like all previous immigration laws, was negative in principle; it simply excluded those who could *not read*. Had it provided for the admission of those who had acquired a certain degree of literacy or who possessed a definite amount of intelligence, it would have made a positive contribution. But this it did not do. In its operation it only required the reading of forty words in any language. What that had to do with selecting desirable workers or with choosing capable and intelligent citizens is more than one can see.

Even in the matter of reducing numbers the Literacy Test accomplished virtually nothing. For what would prevent those who *could* read from filling the ranks of those who could not? And this is precisely what did happen in the early postwar period, as we shall presently see. Of course, the Literacy Test Law was not in operation all by itself sufficiently long to prove its restrictive power, nor have we any way of estimating the number of those who were prevented from embarking for America by the passage of that law. What we do know, however, is that while 250,000 persons were admitted during the fiscal years 1917-19, for instance, only a few over 3,000 were rejected on account of illiteracy. We also know that the Literacy Test did not reduce the proportion coming from southeastern Europe, one of the great objects it had set out to accomplish.

By every possible standard, therefore, the Literacy Test fell short of fulfilling its promises. So true was this that in the sober moments of the after-battle, even those who had been for years the most sanguine supporters of the Test were obliged to look about for some other method for restricting immigration. Thus a vast effort, stretching over a period of more than a quarter of a century, costing the people who knows how many millions of dollars, creating sharp conflicts, and arousing bitter hatred amounted to practically nothing. It was a clean cut example of what gigantic blunders heated propaganda may lead to.

IX

The enactment of the Literacy Test Law did accomplish one thing, however: it sealed the death of the Asylum tradition. The United States in 1917 set out on an entirely new course so far as the free admission of workers from the Old World was concerned. Before this perhaps they were needed, but now this country could at least theoretically do without the aid of Old World workers. So it took the first step toward barring its gates to newcomers. That is the chief significance of the Literacy Test Law of 1917.

A period of more than a hundred years of national

life this country had passed, during which some 33,-
000,000 trans-oceanic laborers had come in. In the
main they had been *asked* to come, protected during
the journey, welcomed on arrival and sought after
when they had landed. Their life blood had produced
at least some of the strong cement of national life.
Things had now changed. The gates were about to
be closed. The Literacy Test Law was but one step
in the general direction. More significant laws were
soon to be enacted with the aim of barring as many
would-be immigrants as possible. Whether this
change will accrue to the good of the worker already
in this country or to the progress of the laborer
the world over, we cannot at this time even guess.
We only know that the Old World laborer could
from now on no longer enter freely.

"At last", wrote one proponent of restriction,
"the demand for the restriction of immigration . . .
has found expression in a measure which ostensibly
completes the selective system of admission, and for
which, by all tests, the people were ready two decades
ago. How long it will take to secure the passage of
a frankly restrictive law . . . time alone can tell."

It is not "time alone" however, that always tells;
nor in the case in point was it time that told. In
the life of nations as in that of individuals, some
catastrophe may in a moment produce changes, far
reaching and portentous, which in the normal
course of human events could not be effected in long

periods of time. In the life of nations, also, some ego-centric theory, propounded in time of national or international stress is capable of precipitating avalanches of so-called patriotic emotions, of swerving a whole people away from constructive effort and of setting a whole nation on paths to which sober thought would not have directed. It was the War that made possible the passing of the immigration act of 1917, and the War that paved the way for the events of 1921-24 in immigration history, to a consideration of which we will now turn.

CHAPTER V

ON THE WAY TO THE CLOSED DOOR

But if war breaks out, the chances are that everybody you admire will begin to feel the justification of
killing and hating. At first the vent of these feelings
is very narrow. . . . Gradually the impulse to kill
becomes the main business . . . [it] becomes central, is sanctified, and gradually turns unmanageable.
It seeks a vent not alone on the idea of the enemy
. . . but upon all persons and objects and ideas
that have always been hateful. . . . It takes a
long time to subdue so powerful an impulse once it
goes loose. And therefore, when war is over in fact,
it takes time and struggle to regain self-control, and
to deal with the problems of peace in civilian character.—*Walter Lippmann.*

I

ON April 6, 1917, fifty-nine days after the Literacy Test had become law, the United States declared
war and a situation arose which severely strained all
the immigration laws of the land. The supply of
labor was already considerably reduced. Comparatively small numbers of immigrants were entering the
country; large numbers had left during the years
1915, 1916 and the early months of 1917. Then
came the mobilization in the United States of millions of men for military and industrial service.

All of these events gave rise to the belief that an

insufficient number of workers existed for the emergency needs of this country. Soon after the declaration of war representations were made to the United States Immigration Bureau, especially by the farmers of the Southwest and there was a dearth of workers. In the spring and summer of 1918 Immigration Officials themselves reported a scarcity of laborers for work on the maintenance of ways and in certain coal mining industries in which the Government was interested on account of their bearing upon the conducting of the war. Accordingly various interests began to cast about for fresh supplies of laborers. Since Europe, the customary labor mine, was closed by the war, both official and unofficial United States turned its eyes toward Porto Rico, the Philippines, the Virgin Islands and some even looked toward Asia.

As a matter of historical fact, however, Mexico and Canada supplied the bulk of laborers who came in during the period the United States was at war. Taking advantage of Clause 9 of Section 3 of the 1917 immigration law, under which the Department of Labor had the power to admit *temporarily* otherwise inadmissible aliens, special executive orders were issued permitting laborers to be brought in from Mexico to supply the demands of the agricultural fields of the Southwest. From and through Canada workers were also imported for the logging camps of Maine, for the shipbuilding industries and for general labor in the various states.

The manner in which many Mexicans were brought and kept in the United States during the War period constitutes a chapter of immigration history of which no thinking American can be proud. In the first place they were induced to come into the country in virtual violations of the contract labor law, the Literacy Test, the head tax and other provisions of the immigration law. Then they were herded like cattle, were *forced* to remain in the localities and on specific "ranches", were forbidden to seek employment or higher wages elsewhere. In some cases their shoes and clothes were taken away from them in order to keep them from escaping. Those who tried to escape were apprehended and forced to return. Those who objected to staying on the "ranch" to which they had been brought or to the treatment they were receiving were arrested and deported. Under this practice at least 50,852 Mexicans were imported by the end of the fiscal year 1920 and this system operated down to March 2, 1921. Here and there a legislator or a labor union did object, but as a whole the practice was permitted with the full knowledge of United States officials and legislators.

II

This movement was centered primarily in the Southwest; elsewhere agitation continued in favor of restriction. In fact restrictionists in the East and South took advantage of the war temper in order to bring about a greater reduction of immigration.

Their first attack made appeal to war hysteria. No sooner had this country declared war than some raised the cry that the foreign born were proving disloyal to this country and its cause. By August the cry had been heard in Congress and made current throughout the country, causing great consternation and distress among our immigrant population. In Congress a number of anti-immigrant bills were introduced, the principal one of which was the famous "alien slackers" bill. This bill was sponsered, it is significant to note, by Mr. Burnett of Alabama, a man who for years had been very active in the anti-immigration movement. So great was the anxiety that the bill should become law in the heat of the moment, that the Committee reported it back to the House in the record time of one day with recommendation that it pass.

Although Congress seemed disinclined to pay attention to the issue, in September Mr. Burnett again pressed the matter. "From all over the country," said his report to the House, "comes the cry of the rank injustice of the forcing of American citizens into the war while alien slackers are here in vast numbers enjoying the peaceful privileges of our country and immunity from fighting for the very integrity of their own countries. . . ." Thousands of Canadians, continued the report, have crossed the

border of the United States for the purpose of evad-
ing the draft of their country, and immigrants from
France have increased from 18,166 in 1914 to 24,-
405 in 1917. They are betraying the country which
has given them hospitality, these immigrants!

Throughout the first and second sessions of the
65th Congress the subject again and again came to
the fore. But Congress refused to pass or even
give respectful attention to the "alien slackers" bill,
so unfounded in fact evidently was the allegation it
implied. The President's order of April 11, 1918,
and the Act of Congress of July 9, 1918, at last
put a stop to this particular movement by making
provisions, in harmony with international law, for
handling the aliens who had refused to participate
in the war.

Since much that followed in immigration legislation may clearly be traced to war hysteria it is
important to inquire at this point: how far was it
true that the foreign born were disloyal? The report
of the Provost Marshal General gives specific
answer. It shows that many declarant aliens *did*
refuse to complete their citizenship in order to evade
military service, that thousands of non-declarants
did claim and receive exemption, while thousands
more sought and obtained their discharge from service after they had been duly inducted.

But the report of the Provost Marshal General
also shows that twenty per cent of the American

Army in the World War was Irish, twelve per cent Italian, and five per cent Jewish; to cite only a few of the nationalities. (*New Republic*, November 2, 1921.)

"Truly," continues the report after citing official facts and figures; "were we the melting pot of the world; and the cosmopolitan composition of our population was never more strikingly disclosed than by the recent events of the world war. Then the melting pot stood in the fierce fires of the national emergency; and its contents, heated in the flames, either fused into the compact mass or floated off as dross. . . .

"No man can peruse the muster roll of one of our camps, or the casualty list from a battlefield in France, without realizing that America has fulfilled one of its highest missions in breeding a spirit of common loyalty among all those who have shared the blessings of life on its free soil. No need to speculate how it has come about; the great fact is demonstrated that America makes Americans.[1]

"The mass of foreign-born residents were . . . permeated by the spirit of readiness to waive their exemptions and voluntarily accept the call to military service. Thousands of non-declarant aliens of co-belligerent and even neutral origin welcome the opportunity to take up arms . . . ; the records of

[1] These official statements and the facts supporting them would seem to refute the contention made by H. P. Fairchild in *The Melting-Pot Mistake.*—The Author.

correspondence in this office contain eloquent testimony to this spirit. The figures of alien classification already given . . . indicate this; and the local boards report explicitly that the number of non-declarant aliens waiving their exemption was very large (191,491). And finally, the figures of naturalizations in camp since May, 1918 . . . refute the notion that any appreciable number of those men had entered the service unwillingly."

Even thousands of persons of German stock, in spite of the distrust which at first attended them in public opinion, stood loyally by the cause of the United States and the Germans gave a large and loyal share of genuine support to the draft.

It seems clear, therefore, that the charge of disloyalty was but the cry of the agitators. So false, in fact, was it that it was not used in the postwar propaganda.

III

Concurrently, however, another line of attack was being made, which *was* to have a great influence upon the American mind. Reference is made to the Nordic-theory movement. The idea had been expounded long before this by Gobineau, Chamberlain and William III of Germany in the form of the super-race theory. But it was left for Madison Grant to devolve it in his book *The Passing of the Great Race* (1916) in such a striking manner as to stir America. His contention briefly stated is that the tall, long-headed, blond, light-eyed people, the so-called Nordics, are the supermen of the earth, all others "scum". The blond men with dark eyes, or the dark short men with light eyes, or the dark-skinned, light-eyed or black . . . are all disharmonic combinations, the unfit and a menace. And since it was the Nordic who won the North American continent from the grip of the wild and gave it western civilization, only that race has a right to it.

But, continued Madison Grant in substance, the Alpines and Mediterraneans, very inferior peoples indeed, have been coming to this country in large numbers in late years. Their coming threatens the very existence of the United States and its people. They breed very rapidly and therefore will attain numerical supremacy. They are low-blood people and their blood infused in America's veins will produce a "mongrel" race. They are incapable of and inexperienced in self-government. Their presence will destroy the American democracy; while their inability to adapt themselves to the life of this country will surely lead to general demoralization and degradation . . . *unless* they are stopped from entering the country.

The amazing extent to which this idea seized the American mind can be gathered from the literature of the time. Being a theory difficult of proof one way or the other it swept whole regions like a gigantic fire, by the momentum of its ego-centric heat. It played an important part in stimulating war time prejudices and in paving the way for restriction.[1]

IV

A third argument which paved the way for immigration restriction was found in the fact that the United States had been able to weather the industrial stress of war without the aid of foreigners.

For the first time, then, tangible evidence was available that America *could*, after all, do without additional foreign laborers. "During the period of the World War," stated a report of the Senate Committee on Immigration, "the European and home orders for munitions and other war material created an abnormal demand upon manufacturing industries of the United States, but during the same period European immigration was almost wholly cut off. . . . During the war period, 1915-1919, inclusive, we admitted substantially no immigrants from Europe. Thus it will be seen that although our industries had so largely increased they were conducted without the 4,000,000 immigrants who would undoubtedly otherwise have been admitted and given employment."

---

[1] An intensely interesting book was published in Portland, Oregon, in 1925: Samuel Albert Brown's *The House of Israel or The Anglo-Saxon,* which "proves" by means of Biblical citations that the "Nordic people" are *the* people of the Lord.

If America's manufacturing industries were able to meet so successfully the extraordinary war time demands without drawing upon further immigrant labor, could they not, now that peace had come, get along without it? Moreover large numbers of native young men who left the countryside during the War still remain in the manufacturing pursuits. Is there, therefore, any real need for additional labor? Thus ran the argument.

To this argument organized Labor lent the weight of its newly acquired strength. The absence of new foreign workers in the American market had enabled Labor to make appreciable net gains in wages, working conditions and organization. This gave it a greater political power so that when time came to consolidate and make permanent its gains, one of Labor's chief concerns was to see to it that immigration should be greatly restricted or stopped altogether for a period of years. Organized Labor's voice now took on a tone of authority and the Secretary of the American Federation of Labor could appear before a Committee of Congress with practically a *demand* for "the prohibition of immigration for a period of not less than two years, and without reservations."

Of course the United States had been able to meet its war time labor needs in part because of the several millions of foreign laborers already in this country. It was the stress of war, the countrywide

organization of employment exchanges, the regulation of seasonal trades, industrial and general training guidance, the systematic reduction of labor turn-
over, the decasualization of labor, the control of
hours and conditions of work that made it possible
for this country to meet the labor requirements of
war, and all these conditions could not be expected
to continue.   But this line of reasoning did not
matter; the United States had been successful in the
war without additional immigrant labor and it *could*
get along without it in peace time also, if it willed.

Another reason for restriction was found in the
great amount of unemployment prevailing in the
postwar period.   In the autumn of 1920 depression
and widespread unemployment began.   The American Federation of Labor found, early in 1921, in
141 cities alone, 1,819,272 workers out of employment.   Representative Johnson stated before the
Senate Committee on Immigration that his findings
showed that in eight counties in Pennsylvania alone
82,500 persons were unemployed; at Denver 10,000
were without employment; in Providence and vicinity,
23,000; at Rochester 26,000; at Omaha, 10,000;
at Kansas City, 15,000; at Newark, 41,000; at St.
Louis, 35,000; at Detroit, between 154,000 and
184,000.   Gordon S. Watkins, in *An Introduction
to the Study of Labor Problems*, estimates that in

June 1921 the number of idle workers was from three and a half to four million, with at least as many more working only part time. In July, 1921, more than 3,900,000 fewer persons were employed in manufacturing and mechanical industries than in January 1920. In August 1921 the United States Bureau of Labor Statistics found that the number of unemployed had reached a total of 5,735,000.

V

The labor and political disturbances of the War and the post war period also made their contribution to the restriction movement. In the years 1916-21 inclusive occurred no less than 19,970 strikes and 625 lock-outs, involving probably 15,000,000 persons directly and 5,000,000 indirectly in the strikes and about 750,000 in the lock-outs.

The one labor disturbance which probably had a direct and important bearing upon immigration-restriction was the Steel Strike of 1919. Although the strikers included all types of workers, Americans, "old" immigrants, "new" ones and all kinds of mixtures, it happened that in the Pittsburgh district most of the strikers were foreign born and unskilled workers. American workmen in that region were not out, in part, because they were under contract and also because they held the skilled jobs with higher pay and better working conditions. This fact created an impression that the strike was the result of radicalism, "Bolshevism" and other "alien" influences. Around Pittsburgh, especially, these "ugly" influences were held responsible for the strike. The average American was stricken with panicky fear of the "foreigner", particularly the "hunkie". The word "alien," having acquired a peculiarly ugly significance during the war, now struck terror into the American mind. (Interchurch World Movement: *Public Opinion and the Steel Strike.*)

The radical movements of the war and early postwar period produced similar results. The antiwar activities of the Non-Partisan League, of Debs, Berger, Mrs. O'Hare and their followers, of W. D. Haywood and the I. W. W. followed as they were by the succeeding outrages of 1919 and by the discovery in the mail of a large number of bombs addressed to Federal officials and judges; the mysterious wrecking by explosion of the houses of Attorney General Palmer and other individuals prominent in sedition legislation and prosecution; the great amount of street fighting in May Day Parades in Boston and Cleveland; the clash of very obscure origin between the I. W. W. and the American Legion in Centralia, Washington, in which four ex-service men were shot to death and one lynched—these and many other minor happenings of similar character threw the American public into a state of hysteria —*all* disturbances were attributed to the influence of aliens.

The legislation of the time bears the imprint of this state of mind. The Espionage Act of 1918, already severe to the extreme, was amended in 1920 so as to include clauses providing for the punishment of defamation of our form of government and the curtailment of production. "A federal Sabotage Act was enacted. States punished the advocacy of syndicalism and sabotage in their war statutes and more often by separate acts. Much of this legislation extended automatically to peace time utterances. . . . In the legislative sessions which followed the armistice, emergency laws against anarchy and criminal syndicalism were adopted by state after state," with surprising coincidence of time and phraseology. (Chafee, *Freedom of Speech.*) Several states created special commissions to investigate radicalism, the most notable of which was the Lusk Committee of New York State. In 1919 a countrywide investigation was conducted by the United States Department of Justice which purported to have discovered large numbers of radical publications in foreign languages and a vast amount of subversive activity all over the country.

This movement was directed primarily against aliens and culminated in what former Assistant Secretary of Labor Louis Post calls *The Deportation Delirium.* This delirium led to the raids of the late months of 1919 and the early days of 1920, and to the arrest, on the authority of about 550 warrants, of some 10,000 foreigners, mostly Russians, who were entirely unprotected on account of the fact that their parent government was completely disorganized. Some of those who were apprehended had been in this country for years, had families and property and were citizens. Many of them were held in prisons under intolerable conditions and not a few of them were deported. The majority of them were later found to be innocent of any connection with radical movements. (Panunzio, *The Deportation Cases of 1919-1920.*)

This delirium, states Mr. Post, who as Assistant Secretary of Labor was in intimate touch with the situation, "derived its distinctive characteristics from reports of mysterious crimes attributed to aliens. . . . The public easily saw anarchy spooks in every shadow. . . . The bombing crimes, real and imaginary alike, were associated in American thought with alien 'reds.' " The word *red* "intended originally to symbolize the world brotherhood of the Apostolic declaration—'of one blood all the nations of men' " was interpreted "as a threat of blood sacrifice. That sinister interpretation was reënforced in the United States with a bitterly patriotic aversion to the red flag as an alien menace to the red-white-and-blue. These mental associations of 'reds' with foreigners, and of 'red' foreigners with destructive conspiracy, were intensified by sensational reports of revolutionary horrors in Soviet Russia where the 'red' flag waved. . . ."

These industrial disturbances and these radical movements, associated as they were with immigrants, produced another important result. They brought employers also, perhaps for the first time in the history of the country, definitely to the side of the restrictionist. That section of American population which may, roughly, be described as the capitalistic class, until 1914 were sentimentally, theoretically and for "personal" reasons in favor of unrestricted immigration. Now their attitude changed. They saw in the foreigners, especially in the peoples of central, southern and eastern Europe, who had supplied the largest increment to foreign labor in this country in late years, not only people extremely difficult of assimilation, but also importers of "anarchistic" and "radical" doctrines. If permitted to come in large numbers they might possibly overthrow the government and the capitalistic system. Therefore they must be restricted, perhaps entirely barred out.[1]

VI

To add to this jumble of fears, rumors spread widely, (no doubt with some foundation in fact, so far as numbers were concerned,) that millions of immigrants of "the poorest and most refractory sort" were "almost literally standing in line at European seaports waiting for ships to bring them over." From

[1] Later they again reverted to their original position.

Czechoslovakia, England, Italy, the Netherlands, Serbia and Spain, Turkey and Poland reports came from consular officers that millions were awaiting transportation facilities to carry them to the United States. The Commissioner of Immigration for the Port of New York gave it as his estimate that Italy was preparing to send five millions of her people to the United States, and Germany eight millions, and that five million European emigrants were already "packed", ready to leave their old homes for America. The Commissioner General of Immigration was quoted as saying that "from ten to twenty-five million Europeans were ready to come to the United States"—and these reports were circulated widely and subsequently submitted as evidence in the hearings of the Senate Committee on Immigration. (*New York Herald*, Jan. 3, 1921.)

VII

And in 1919 and 1920 Old World laborers, stimulated no doubt by rumors that America was about to close its gates to all comers, did begin to arrive in increasing numbers, (141,132 in fiscal year 1919, 430,001 in 1920, and 805,228 in 1921). Everywhere the fear was expressed that America was in danger, that an emergency existed, and the demand was made that something needed to be done and done *quickly*.

The records of the time clearly reflect the anxiety all these movements produced. From January 28,

1919 to June 5, 1920, no less than *ten bills* were introduced in Congress, nine in the House and one in the Senate.   Three provided for suspension of immigration for two years, one for three years, three for four years, and two for a period of ten years or more.   The Senate bill provided for the suspension of immigration from every source for a period of *twenty years* and from Germany, Austria, Hungary, Bulgaria and Turkey for *fifty years*.   The House, always in the vanguard in such matters, passed a bill, on December 13, 1920, by a vote of 295 to 41, providing that immigration should be suspended altogether for two years.   The Senate Committee on Immigration took a calmer view.   The emergency it saw was that there was "a general desire upon the part of the younger and more enterprising men in the nations of eastern and southern Europe to better their condition by coming to the United States. . . . It was the new immigration coming in unprecedented numbers which created our prewar problem and . . . it is the impending return of this movement to its prewar status which, in the opinion of the committee, constitutes the present emergency."   To care for this emergency the Committee recommended that instead of suspending immigration altogether that a method be devised by which immigration should be held down and preference be given to northern and western Europeans.   To this end the per centum principle, later incorporated in the law, was advocated.

The House Committee on Immigration and naturalization insisted that a drastic law should be enacted and right early. On January 14, 1921, Representative Albert Johnson of Washington, chairman of the Committee, speaking before the House declared: "Many predicted a great influx, and in July of last year it began—50,000 to 70,000 a month—and it still continues in spite of the most tremendous handicaps that immigrants have ever known. Steerage rates at $100 to $120; a head tax of $8.00; requirements of a passport and a United States vise on same, the vise alone costing $10.00— and in the countries of central Europe aliens stand in line by the week before our consular offices in the effort to secure the vise, which permits them to start for the land of promise. . . . In my opinion the remaining months of this year will see each month's quota of immigrants run around 100,000.

"If admitted, they find no houses ready for them, and are thrown into the tenements already over-crowded with others of their nationalities, and in every such house lives an alien enemy of this Government who is preaching its overthrow and handing out revolutionary circulars printed in the language of the newly arrived. Opportunity for immediate gain is the goal sought by so many immigrants and in the present conditions of our cities that opportunity is non-existent and discontent follows, which is easily fanned into flames of revolution by paid agitators, who are at their dirty work night and day, with such circulars as the one I hold here, entitled 'fill the jails', or such banners as this one, emblazoned in gold on a red background, 'The Soviet Program.' What do these foreigners know of government by the people? The first time the school health officer sends the little 6-year-old immigrant boy home to be washed up the mother thinks that the whole Government of the United States is closing in on her. What does she know about government with the consent of the governed?

"And the revolutionary agitator is on the corner mouthing his piece about the theories of Karl Marx, and lauding the dream of the dictatorship of the proletariat. Her man loses his job, and he is disconsolate. There is the agitator, and the Soviet workers' hall just around the corner. He joins. The mother goes to work in a sweat shop. She provides, even though wages fall. Her children suffer and they go to the meetings where they drink in the dream of a general strike."

And a month or so later—a few cases of vermin-infested immigrants and one case of typhus having been discovered among those arriving—Representative Albert Johnson of Washington introduced remarks into the House under the caption *Danger, Disease and Death Come with Present Immigration.*

VIII

Thus the stage was set for the Act of 1921. Millions of Old World laborers already in this country, thousands of them unemployed and causing industrial and political disturbances, millions actually standing, like a vast and hungry throng, upon the shores of southeastern Europe ready to dash across the ocean the moment transportation facilities were available.[1] In those who fain would come lurks danger, disease and death! By far the larger portion of them are poor of the poorest. Dependents, rather than producers, deficient, defective and delinquent rather than normal. The accommodations at United States receiving stations are wholly inadequate to examine them properly. The shortage of housing is such that if large numbers are admitted they will only go to swell the hordes of the dreaded hovels of the slums. Above all in both those who are here and those who are coming are deposited the explosives of Bolshevism, radicalism, anarchism, which will surely overthrow the Government of the United States! The danger is imminent! Act, Congress! Act quickly!

And Congress did act. A bill, limiting the number of immigrants to 3 per cent of the foreign born in this country in 1910, passed both Houses during February, 1921. But President Wilson pocket-vetoed it. The measure, virtually unchanged, was reintroduced in the early days of the next Congress, passed the House without a roll call on April 22, 1921, the Senate all but for one vote unanimously, on

[1] Transportation facilities for 1,500,000 a year were available.

May 3, and by the signature of the President it
became law on May 19, 1921. Thus President
Harding goes down into history as the first Chief
Executive to set his official approval upon a general
legislative act which all but closed the gates of one
portion of the world to the laborers of another. It
needs to be added, however, that the *Three Per
Centum Limit Act*, as that law came to be known,
was enacted expressly for one year and specifically
as an emergency measure.

Speaking generally, the Act of May 19, 1921,
departed from all previous immigration laws of the
United States in two major respects: first, it set a
specific limit upon the number of those to be admitted, and second, it took the first definite step in the
direction of selection by "racial" preference.[1]

The fundamental principle remained the same,
viz: selection by rejection. The *Three Per Centum
Limit Act* indirectly added certain "racial" groups
to all the previously enumerated classes subject to
exclusion thereby perpetuating the principle introduced by, and active in immigration legislation since,
the law of 1882.

To what extent the *Three Per Centum Limit Act*
actually reduced numbers will be discussed in the next
chapter. Here it needs to be stressed that so great

[1] The Literacy Test law aimed to produce this same result
but not with such definite numerical limitations as was the
case with the Act of 1921.

was the sense of impending doom under which the legislators were working at the time that they gave the world only a *two-weeks' notice*. Even the Literacy Test Law, a much less drastic law, went into effect ninety days after enactment. But the law of 1921 became effective on June 3, just *fifteen days* after it had received executive approval; and this gave rise to a racing of laborer-laden ships across the ocean, the like of which had never been seen before and may never be seen again.

CHAPTER VI

THE RACE OF RACES

Beyond the ocean stretches lay a Land young and bold, dreamed of youth and of old, the home of the needy, a place of safe refuge. Toward it bent the weary mass of men, weary of strife, saddened with persecution. The ships raced across the sea, into the channel marked by the blazoning hand of Liberty. But behind Her, great bars held back the dreaming travelers and back they turned, back to the Old World, to hope and dream no more.—*Mark Elder.*

I

Two giant steamers left a Greek port on the same day, both bound for New York, both expecting to reach that harbor by the first day of the new month. Their passengers were nearly all Greek subjects, who like all migrants, had broken home ties, gone through the period of waiting for passage, and doubtless staked their all in the hope of coming to the Promised Land. Perhaps they had heard vague rumors about a law, recently passed, which limited the number of immigrants admissible to the United States. But how could they turn back now?

The two steamers followed the usual course and being of approximately equal speed reached America at about the same time. They hovered about at the edge of the three mile limit, their boilers surcharged with steam, their funnels belching out massive columns of smoke and burning cinders into the black night; they awaited the sound of the last stroke of the midnight bell which would usher in the new month and with it the new monthly quota. One may well imagine how expectantly the mass of human faces on the decks looked out toward Liberty and the city of many towers.

At the sound of the midnight bell the steamers started forward with a leap; they raced through the Ambrose Channel, down into New York harbor, toward the Statue of Liberty. One ship, however, reached quarantine *two minutes* ahead of the other, with enough immigrants to fill a whole month's quota for Greece. *They* were admitted! And the Greeks on board the second steamer—every one of them was debarred and sent back to Europe!

This incident, taken substantially from Professor Davie's *A Constructive Immigration Policy*, and supplemented from the testimony of the Commissioner General of Immigration before the House Committee on Immigration and Naturalization, is but one of the many races of immigrant-laden ships which occurred after the passage of the 1921 immigration law. Since the law provided that twenty per cent of the annual quota were admissible during any one month steamers raced madly in order to reach the various United States ports the very first hours of the first day of each of the first five months of the fiscal year.

For nearly three years this racing continued. "It is not an uncommon sight," said Senator Reed of Pennsylvania before the Senate in 1924, "to see 15 liners racing for New York harbor to try to get there at one minute past 12 o'clock, each trying to get ahead of all the others. . . .

"At first the goal was the quarantine station on Staten Island, and we actually had the spectacle of great ocean liners racing each other neck and neck through the Ambrose Channel. . . . It was obvious that if they kept that up there was going to be a bad wreck sooner or later, and so . . . [it was] announced that the goal would be the lightship at the entrance of the harbor; that when the [steamers] go to that point their order of examination would be determined, and they did not need to race within New York harbor. But there is still this phenomenon of racing at the beginning of each of the first five months of the fiscal year, and it is entirely unintelligent, and it is entirely unfair to the immigrant who is excluded. It is not at all his fault that his boat loses in the race; and yet, as the result of it, he is apt to be deported and barred from return for nearly a year."

The fate of Old World workers who sought to

come to this country lay no longer in inherent capacity, personal merit, initiative or choice; no longer in whether or not they were worthy of the opportunity America offers newcomers; it lay rather in horse power—the speed capacity of steamers. The very moment of the ship's arrival determined the life outcome of hundreds, perhaps thousands of individuals.

How many immigrants arrived during the years 1921-24 in excess of quotas and were debarred for that reason only is not and may never be known. We do know, however, that during the first twenty-seven days the 1921 law was in operation, that is from June 3 to 30, more than 10,000 aliens arrived at United States ports *in excess of quotas.* Ellis Island became greatly congested, the immigrants were huddled together, the immigration machinery was badly clogged and the law itself was put to a severe test. These 10,000 excess-quota immigrants just mentioned, however, were admitted by executive order; and during Christmas week of 1921, 1000 more immigrants were permitted to enter, as an act of Christmas good will. By the end of 1921, 2680 persons were deported for the sole reason that they were in excess of quota and during the fiscal year 1923-24 over 10,000 reached in excess of quota, of whom only 500—how selected no one knows—were actually deported.

"The height of absurdity and extraordinary hardship" writes Professor Davie in the work mentioned, "seems to have been reached in the case of some immigrants who arrived on June 30, 1922, the date of the ending of the fiscal year, a few hours before the new quotas for another fiscal year would be available. They were counted as having arrived in the old year after the quota was filled and were required, in order to gain admission, to return to the old country and then come back again and make another application under the new quota."

In individual cases also the application of the law gave rise to serious difficulties. "An immigrant arrived who had been born in Australia of English parents, while the latter were merely visiting there. This immigrant had lived in Australia but six months and had come here from England; nevertheless, she was debarred because the Australian quota was exhausted. A French woman arrived with her son who had been born in the Seychelles Islands, off the east coast of Africa, while his father, now dead, was practising law there. Under the quota system the Seychelles Islands are classed as African and the quota for Africa was expended when they arrived. As a consequence, the woman found that in the eyes of the law her son was of a different nationality than either his French father or herself. She was permitted to enter, since the French quota was not completed, but her son was denied that permission on the ground that the African quota was already filled."

As usual, no one wished to assume responsibility

for a situation generally recognized as one of the most absurd ever developed in the history of civilized nations. The Commissioner General of Immigration attributed it "in part (to) the eagerness of the aliens themselves to get in before the gates were closed, and in part (to) the efforts of competing steamship lines to carry as much as possible of the limited immigrant business. . . . The latter seems to have been by far the more important factor." The real cause may be found in hysterical propaganda and in the haste with which the 1921 act was passed, approved and put into operation.

II

And now the Smyrna disaster occurred, as if some strange power was bringing a test case before the Tribunal of History, to determine whether or not America had actually ceased to exist as the Promised Land. In September 1922, the Turkish Army took Smyrna and the city turned into sheets of flames. The people were surrounded by a vicious triangle of flames on one side, the Turkish army on the second and the sea on the third. The helpless, maddened throngs pressed hopelessly toward the waters. Great numbers were taken aboard the foreign ships in the harbor.

In the weeks following more than a million [1] persons found themselves homeless and countryless.

[1] The most conservative estimate. See *Monthly Summary* of the League of Nations, Supplement 1924.

Since the Turkish authorities drove all men of
military age toward the interior, the refugees
were for the most part women, children and aged
persons—doubly helpless. As many as possible were
taken to the islands of the Aegean and the Grecian
mainland. In two days alone 74,000 were removed.
The four United States destroyers, which were in
the waters, together with the ships of other nations,
did what they could. Great congestion, however,
resulted, especially on the islands of Mytilene and
Chios, where their number was placed at 400,000 and
where they ran the risk of wholesale starvation.

The American people, always keenly responsive to
the suffering arising from any disaster, were moved.
With characteristic dispatch, they sent clothing,
food and shelter. The American Red Cross alone
expended $3,000,000 in relief work during the eight
months following the disaster; and thus the American
people, as a report of the League of Nations put it,
"added another chapter to their already long record
of great acts of charity."

But more than charity, what the Smyrna refugees,
like all persecuted people evidently sought was a
home, a New World, and a chance to start life anew.
They turned their footsteps toward the various
European countries and were admitted in considerable numbers; Greece alone, according to the League
of Nations, took in more than a million and a half.

Some turned their faces toward this country. And this perhaps was natural. America had for two centuries been a refuge for the oppressed. Then, also, many had relatives here and therefore sought to join them. But the United States had adopted a quota law, under which only 5,682 could be admitted from Greece and Turkey combined for the fiscal year 1922-23. (Greek quota 3,294 and Turkish 2,388, including the Smyrna and Turkish-Armenian regions). The quotas, moreover, were already exhausted, so that *not even one* refugee could be legally admitted.

The American public rose to the situation and was clearly moved to act with generosity in the face of the emergency. Prominent individuals and representatives of organizations appeared before the House Committee on Immigration and Naturalization during the week preceding Christmas 1922. They pleaded not for the wholesale admission of refugees, but rather, for the entrance of *only those who had blood relatives* in this country, who were citizens or declarants and could *guarantee* that the refugees would not become public charges.

Among those appearing before the Committee were such persons as Professor Ellsworth Huntington of Yale, Professor Edward Capps of Princeton University and Dr. Esther Lovejoy, chairman of the Executive Board of American Women's Hospitals. The organizations which sent representatives or memorials included the American Legion, the Ameri-

can Federation of Labor, the Federal Council of
Churches, the Near East Relief Committee, the Con-
ference on Immigration Policy, the Young Men's
Christian Association, the Young Women's Christian
Association, the Congregational Home Missionary
Society, the Bishops of the Episcopal Church. Gov-
ernment officials: Mr. George Horton, United States
Consul General in charge of the Smyrna district,
Commissioner General of Immigration W. W. Hus-
band, A. W. Dulles, chief of the Division of Near
Eastern Affairs of the United States Department of
States also appeared before the Committee and pre-
sented official evidence showing the grave situation
the Smyrna disaster had created.

The burden of the pleas was that the United States
should temper law with mercy and admit at least the
relatives of United States citizens, capable of supporting the refugees. Professor Capps of Princeton
University in discussing the bill then before Congress
said: "My impression is that it will not go very far
as a measure of relief; but it will be a very great
relief to a limited number of families who are in very
great distress because of their relatives in Thrace
and the Near East. However, it would surprise me
if, in conformity with these regulations, more than
10,000 to 15,000 should come in; and I should think,
too, that the quality of the immigrants that you
would get through these restrictions [admitting only
blood relatives of citizens and declarants who had

sufficient means to give guarantees] would be the
best; that is, men and women of substance, whose
relatives on this side have an acknowledged position
and are reputable citizens. So that I think that you
have very properly guarded the quality and numbers
of those who may come in.

"Personally, I regret very much to see any restriction placed by this country against the victims of
the very great disaster that is going on in Asia,
because we are the only country in the world (are
we not?) that closes its doors to a person who is suddenly driven out of his house and home. . . ."

In the Senate, Senators Wadsworth of New York
and Sterling of South Dakota presented communications signed by a number of organizations pleading
for the admission of the refugees. Senator Walsh of
Massachusetts offered a resolution on December 5,
1922, to amend the immigration law. Even Senator
Lodge was in favor of offering relief to the refugees.
Early in January 1923 the Senate Committee on
Immigration presented a report recommending the
passage of Bill 4092 which provided for the admission of Armenian refugees, stating that these were
"a race without a national home" a people "highly
literate, and both in intelligence and assimilability
. . . far in advance of other immigrants from southeastern Europe and Asia Minor."

A few days later Senator Robinson of Arkansas said in the Senate: "Whatever may be the details, the world knows that all forms of violence, both to persons and property—arson, robbery, torture, rape, and murder—have converted Smyrna and its vicinity into a realm where brutal barbarism is supreme. The least that the United States can do is to afford refuge for the oppressed, and to act quickly. To delay the consideration and passage of the Armenian refugee bill to consider measures like the ship subsidy or general immigration legislation seems to me unjustifiable, not to say unpardonable. The sentiment of a Christian Nation revolts at the thought that the Congress of the United States should pursue a policy of indifference and hesitation respecting such a subject. The people are hopeful now that we will act promptly and effectively. They will be righteously indignant if we fail and leave Armenian Christians to a fate pitiable beyond the power of the imagination to conceive or the tongue to describe."

But in the lower House every proposal to render the refugees relief was vigorously fought, particularly by Albert Johnson of Washington. The picture which the opponents saw was again one of impending doom.

It is worthy of special note that Lothrop Stoddard was the principal person who appeared before the House Committee on Immigration and Naturalization opposing the admission of the refugees. Mr. Stoddard had just returned from a brief visit to the Near East with reports regarding the people and the political situation in those parts, and this is the picture he presented:

They are Levantines, he said, "the result of an extraordinary racial mixture which has been going on for at least 2,000 years. They have certain characteristics which are recognizable, not only in modern times, but in ancient times, and these characteristics, many of them, are extremely undesirable.

"In my opinion, there is going to be a continuance of trouble here, throughout the Near East. . . . Twenty to twenty-five millions will be refugees within the course of a generation, very probably within the next ten years. . . . I can conceive of no more undesirable type of immigrants than they would be."

These remarks, specious, vague and in the nature of personal opinion as they may be considered, nevertheless painted a gloomy picture indeed. A disaster would overtake the United States were any of the Smyrna refugees to be admitted. He maintained also that in the wake of those who would be admitted would sooner or later come the unhappy, oppressed, persecuted, homeless, and starving of other lands. With them also would come the very causes that brought them ruin!

This picture was passed on to the House. The bill then before that body, providing for the admission of the refugees, was vigorously fought. A counter proposal was made that the next year's quota amounting to about 6,000 (Greece 3,294 and Turkey including the Smyrna and Turkish-Armenian regions 2,388) be allowed. Mr. Johnson said: "I am proposing to go as far as I think that the United States dare go in the face of this tremendous situation, where millions of people are moving, either through persecution or in search of food and shelter." Parliamentary tactics were resorted to; a general immigration bill was substituted, in spite of the fact that the law of 1921 had been extended to June 30, 1924, and the 67th Congress adjourned without giving any relief whatever to the Smyrna refugees.

The American people by all tokens were clearly anxious to extend a helping hand to the specified refugee. Even Senator Lodge who, as we have seen, had for years stood for rigid restriction, favored leniency in this case. The people, not in effective control of the machinery of government, had their will thwarted and their altruism stunted into inaction principally by three individuals in the House of Representatives. It is interesting also to note that all three of them were from the Far West, one from

Washington, one from California and the other from Texas.

Whatever may have been the forces at play, whoever was responsible or not responsible for refusing admission to the refugees, one thing is certain: America as the land of opportunity for persons of other lands was gradually becoming a thing of the past and whether for good or ill perhaps to return no more!

III

During this time, that is from the latter part of 1921 on, a number of agencies and forces, arisen out of the tumult and hates of war, were giving concrete expression to the fact just mentioned. Chief among these was the Ku Klux Klan, which, it needs to be noticed, was reaching the peak of its power at precisely this time, that is, the latter part of 1922. Claiming and perhaps actually intending to be a fraternal and patriotic organization, in actual operation the Klan turned out to be an organ for "exploiting the hates and prejudices rampant in the post-war period"; (Mecklin: *The Ku Klux Klan.*) As it actually worked out this brotherhood had an abundance of hood but very little of the brother in it.

The Nordic doctrine also was gaining great popularity and becoming a powerful stimulant in American life. Popular books, such as Charles W. Gould's

America A Family Matter, William McDougall's *Is America Safe for Democracy?*, Lothrop Stoddard's *The Rising Tide of Color, The Revolt Against Civilization*, and several others of the same type, were published during the years of 1921 to 1924, and were widely read. These, together with a veritable avalanche of newspaper and magazine articles, all told the same story: that the immigrant, especially the recent immigrant, the immigrant from southern and eastern Europe, was an economic, social and racial menace. R. H. Tawney, the noted English economist, on visiting the United States wrote (in 1924): "My own experience is that I heard more about Anglo-Saxons in the four delightful months which I passed in the United States than I had heard during forty years in the humid island which the barbarians in question were foolish enough to colonize."

Widespread attacks followed, such as that of the *Dearborn Independent* upon the Jews.[1] Peculiar controversies took place, such as the one between the Nordics and the Latins in which each group claimed the honor of having discovered America—a controversy which it is interesting to note, is being revived every October 12. Immigrants or the children of immigrants turned against their own people, as in the case of the vituperative attack made by Gino Speranza in the *World's Work*. Immigrants

[1] Apologies were made by Henry Ford for these attacks upon the Jews, in 1927.

were categorically and continuously assailed, and life became difficult and heart-rending even to the best of them.

During these same years a famous investigation was also made, which is important not only for the notoriety it has attained, but also because it shows how scientific method is sometimes used by legislators. Evidently realizing, as early as 1920, that there were no scientific data with which to substantiate the sweeping generalizations regarding the inferiority of southeastern Europeans, the House Committee on Immigration and Naturalization had secured the services of a "scientist" as "expert eugenics agent" of the Committee. This agent made a study of the inmates of 445 eleemosynary and correctional institutions and presented his findings at a hearing of the Committee in November 1922. His findings "proved conclusively" [sic] the social inadequacy of southeast European immigrants.

The Laughlin report, or "Expert Analysis of the Metal and the Dross in America's Melting Pot", as it was named by the Chairman of the Committee, Albert Johnson of Washington, was found shot through with grossest fallacies. A number of authorities made and published careful studies of it, notably Professor H. S. Jennings, noted naturalist of Johns Hopkins University, in *The Survey* of

December 15, 1923; Professor Joseph M. Gillman, of the University of Pittsburgh, in *The American Journal of Sociology*, of August 1924, and the booklet *Social Adequacy of Foreign Nationals in the United States*, published as Special Report 28 of the National Industrial Conference Board. These studies showed that the Laughlin investigation had failed to make a representative territorial selection of data, that the data had been misrepresented by means of an arbitrarily determined "quota." They showed also that Dr. Laughlin's own conclusions were at great variance with his findings, that he had not made the corrections necessary as to age and sex distribution, that he had assumed what is far from proven (the inheritability of certain defects or states) and that he had failed to take into consideration other well established facts having a direct bearing upon the investigation.

Mr. Lutz of the National Industrial Conference Board appeared before the House Committee on Immigration and Naturalization and presented a study of the report in which he showed that according to the report "among native whites feeble-mindedness is eight times as common as it is among negroes; epilepsy nearly ten times as common, and blindness twenty-four times as common. The tuberculosis rate is 148 per cent higher among whites than among negroes, insanity 57 per cent higher, and deafness 43 per cent higher. The number of deformed is nearly eight times as great, relatively, among native whites as among negroes; and white dependents, in proportion to population, out-number negro dependents four to one. On only one count— crime—does the quota fulfillment of the negroes exceed that of the whites."

In short the Laughlin report was found by competent students and statistical experts to be thoroughly unsound in method and in results obtained and at best it represents, in the words of Dr. Gillman, an attempt on the part of the investigator, "to conceal his preconceptions in the elusiveness of technical statistical inaccuracies."

Fallacious as it was found to be, however, the report has had a great influence. The House Committee on Immigration, which had originally employed the "expert eugenics agent", found in it the necessary ammunition for further and more restrictive legislation. Magazines and newspapers actually fattened with the good news: Recent immigrants were at last *scientifically* proven to be socially inadequate. The *Literary Digest* carried to its millions a chart directly based upon the Laughlin report and bearing the caption "Human Wreckage in the Quotas" (February 23, 1924). In fact it is difficult to estimate the influence the report has had and may still have, for it is mentioned approvingly here and there even by otherwise discriminating persons and even finds a place in such an excellent work

as Fairchild's *Immigration* with the surprising statement that the Laughlin report is "an exceptionally
thorough and scientific study."   (Revised edition, p.
314.)

IV

All these events were paving the way for the enactment of a new immigration law.   In the meantime
the *Three Percentum Limit Act*, as the 1921 law
was officially known, had been extended (May 11,
1922) to June 30, 1924.   Before discussing the 1924
law, however, we may examine the results the 1921
law produced.

It will be recalled that that law was enacted for
the purpose of (1) greatly reducing numbers and
(2) cutting down the proportion of immigrants
from southeastern Europe.   Quotas were allotted on
the basis of 3 per cent of the nationals of the different countries residing in the United States in 1910.
These quotas in the aggregate amounted to 356,995
for 1921-22 and with minor corrections to 357,803
for the other two years.   And it was expected that
immigration would be kept down to about those
figures.

On first examining the figures it appears that the
number of immigrants was considerably reduced,
since only 243,953 immigrant aliens were admitted
in 1921-22, 335,480 in 1922-23, and 357,642 in
1923-24.   These figures, however, show only those

admitted *under the quotas* and not total immigration.   The total number of immigrants admitted,
instead of being about 358,000 amounted to 309,556
in 1921-22, 522,919 for the next year and to
706,896 for 1923-24. So that in the year last mentioned the number actually admitted was almost
twice as great as that provided for in the quotas.

The difference between the quotas and the number
admitted is accounted for in two ways.   First, that
law exempted from the application of the quota all
contiguous territories: Mexico, Canada and the rest
of the New World; so that most of those who entered
this country from contiguous territory were not
counted as quota immigrants.   In 1922-23, for
example,   117,001   entered   from   British   North
America and 63,768 from Mexico; while in 1923-24
200,690 came in from the former and 89,336 from
the latter as non-quota immigrants.

Second, the difference between the aggregate
quotas and the number admitted during 1921-24 is
explained by the fact that the 1921 law, like all previous immigration laws, made numerous exceptions.
Certain classes of aliens were counted against the
yearly or monthly quotas so long as the quotas were
not exhausted, but were admitted in any event after
the quotas were exhausted.   These included aliens
returning from a temporary visit abroad, professional actors, artists, lecturers, professors in colleges
or seminaries, others belonging to the recognized pro-

fessions, as well as domestic servants. Under these various exceptions a not inconsiderable number came in. Thus, to cite one case, while the quota for Italy was 42,057, the number of Italians actually admitted during 1924 amounted to 59,209—the difference being due largely to the exceptions just mentioned.

In order correctly to ascertain the extent to which the 1921 law actually reduced the number of immigrants admitted we need also to consider the number of those *leaving the country*. For, obviously, if large numbers come in and proportionately large numbers go out, the net results, numerically speaking, is the same as when a comparatively small number enters and a proportionately smaller number goes out. The records show that emigration steadily decreased from 198,712 in 1921-22, to 81,450 for 1922-23, and 76,789 for 1923-24. Subtracting emigration from immigration we have what is called net immigration, that is, the real addition to the population by the incoming of outsiders. This *net immigration* amounted to 110,844 for 1921-22, 441,469 for the next year and 630,107 for 1923-24.

Nor does this tell the entire story, for if a law keeps down the number of legal entries and at the same time stimulates the illegal flow, it produces no appreciable reduction; since it is obvious that it matters not—from the point of view of numbers— whether a person enters through the legal channels or not, the result is the same: one more has entered.

It follows, therefore, that correctly to gauge the restrictive value of the 1921 law we need to take into account those entering the country clandestinely.

To ascertain the number of surreptitious entrants is, obviously, a difficult task. With regard to one group, the *seamen*, we do have some authoritative information. The Commissioner General of Immigration reports that the number of seamen *known* to have deserted at United States ports increased considerably during the years under discussion: from 5,879 in 1921-22, to 23,194 for the next year and to 34,679 for 1923-24.

In addition there are the *general illegal entrants*. The exact number of these, by the very nature of the case, cannot be ascertained. Various estimates have been made by United States officials, varying all the way from 78,000 to 350,000. These estimates are based upon certain computations made with reference to those who once in the country seek permits to reënter legally, the number of illegal entry cases coming up in courts, as well as of those who are actually apprehended as illegal entrants. So that while the exact number cannot be discovered, officials can form an idea.

That the number is great is seen from a number of interesting facts. For example, while previous to the enactment of the 1921 law, official reports rarely mention illegal entries—save in the case of Orientals —in recent years the reports of the Commissioner

General of Immigration devote considerable space
and attention to the discussion of the situation, and
even photographs of the Immigration Service Border Patrol are reproduced. Congress, moreover, is
appropriating $1,000,000 a year solely for the pur-
pose of border patrol, in addition to other appropriations made for the same purpose. In addition it
is well known that some Courts, notably the one in
the Northern Judicial District of New York, were
for a time actually deluged with illegal entry cases.
Taking everything into consideration, therefore, and
keeping closely to the lowest estimates, it is safe to
rely on the estimate made by Mr. E. J. Henning, then
Assistant Secretary of Labor, before the Academy of
Political Science in December 1923, that the number
of surreptitious entrants amounted to about 100,000
a year.

When we take all these factors into consideration
and tentatively adopt the conservative estimate of
surreptitious entries, we have what may be called
total corrected immigration under the 1921 law:

TOTAL CORRECTED IMMIGRATION UNDER THREE PER CENTUM
LIMIT ACT.

Fiscal Years Ending June 30

Fiscal Year	Imm. Aliens	− Emig. Aliens	= Net Imm.	+ Desert. Seamen	+ Ill. Entries	= Total Cor. Imm.
1922	309,556	198,712	110,844	5,879	100,000	216,723
1923	522,919	81,450	441,469	23,194	100,000	564,663
1924	706,896	76,789	630,107	34,679	100,000	764,786

These figures would seem to indicate that the *Three Per Centum Limit Act* of 1921 did not produce the permanent reduction in immigration intended. With each year net immigration tended to approach the prewar volume, so that by 1923-24 the permanent addition to our foreign born population was approximately equal to that of the annual increment of the years 1908-14.

If we examine the figures of 1923-24 by themselves this fact will stand out even more clearly. Total immigration for that year was 706,896, emigration was 76,789, thus leaving a net immigration of 630,107. When to this number are added the 34,679 seamen *known* to have deserted and the low estimate of 100,000 surreptitious entrants we have a corrected immigration of 764,786 for 1923-24 or 91,131 more than the yearly average for 1908-14. And even if the estimated 100,000 surreptitious entries are entirely stricken off, and even if one-half of the deserted seamen or 17,500—a *very* generous allowance—are charged off to possible reshipping foreign we still have in 1923-24 a net immigration of 647,286, or practically the same as the average net yearly immigration (673,655) for the years 1908-14. In fact the Commissioner General of Immigration called attention to the fact that "while the number of aliens of both classes admitted in the year just ended (1923-24) was exceeded in 8 of the 17 years considered (1908-23), the permanent addition to the alien population was numerically larger in 1923-24 than in any other year except 1910, 1913, 1914." (*Report*, 1924.)

This fact becomes all the more significant when it is remembered that immigration in prewar years was practically free, not even the Literacy Test Law had been enacted, whereas those entering in 1923-24 did so under a most restrictive law. It needs to be borne in mind, however, that had not the 1921 law been in operation the immigration movement might possibly have increased greatly. Had that been the case, however, the movement out of this country would in all probability have increased proportionately, as the history of immigration would seem to point out. Immigration from contiguous territory, moreover, in all probability would have been proportionately less, while the number of surreptitious entrants would have remained as negligible as before the war; with the net result that the permanent addition to the alien population would have been approximately equal to that which was actually made under the law of 1921.

The 1921 law, however, did produce a greatly increased stability or permanence in immigration, although, as the Commissioner General of Immigration states, "it cannot be said that the law is the only cause that contributed to that end." But even this permanence, if produced by the 1921 law, is a doubtful good from the viewpoint of labor, since a greater permanence would seem to cause greater competition to the laborers already in this country, and therefore largely destroy one of the larger objectives of restriction.

If the data available are even relatively correct, they would seem to point to the general conclusion that artificial restriction has very little effect upon the movement of peoples. At present we do not have sufficiently comprehensive data, covering a broad enough period, to warrant general conclusions; but what data we do have seem to point to the inference that if the movement of population is to be controlled—assuring that this is desirable—we must seek more basic changes than restriction laws produce.

V

As a second large objective, the 1921 law sought to effect a proportionate increase in the immigration from northwestern Europe and a corresponding decrease in that from southeastern Europe. This the law accomplished. Whereas in 1920-21 northwestern Europeans contributed but 25.7 per cent of total immigration, in 1923-24 their proportion had risen to 55.7 per cent; in the same period the people admitted from southern and southeastern Europe and Turkey had decreased from 66.7 to 27.2 per cent of the whole. Numerically expressed between 1921-22 and 1923-24, there was an increase of 186,347 in the first group and a decrease of 344,545 in the second.

It is interesting to note in this connection that the number of Mexicans entering this country increased from 18,246 in 1921-1922, to 62,709 in 1922-23 and to 87,648 in 1923-24, making a total for the three fiscal years of 168,603. Whereas Mexicans constituted but 3.7 per cent of total immigration in 1920-21, their percentage rose to 12.4 in 1923-24. In the last mentioned year their number was equal to about 45 per cent of the year's total immigration of southern and eastern people.

This considerable increase of Mexicans gives rise to two observations. First, with all due regard for the excellent qualities of the Mexicans, it is at best doubtful whether they have as much to contribute industrially, racially or culturally to the development of the United States as have the Jews, for instance, or the Greeks and Italians, who have centuries of civilization experience behind them, but who were largely excluded by the 1921 law, while Mexicans were left practically unrestricted.

In the second place, as it was often observed in the course of recent Congressional discussion, was the vigorous support of the 1921 law given by the West Coast and Southwest in any measure due to sectional interest? This law, by shutting off—at least in intent—large numbers of immigrants from Europe and by permitting a practically unlimited immigration of Mexicans, only served, it was pointed out, to diminish the labor supply of the East and to increase it in the West, since approximately 60 per cent of all Mexican immigrants remain in the West and Southwest.

VI

As already indicated the *Three Per Centum Limit Act of 1921* was to expire on June 30, 1924. Legislators therefore made ready for a new law. From the very first the foregone conclusion was that the new legislation would be at least as restrictive as the one about to die and that it would use the method employed in the 1921 law.

The protagonists of restriction, however, wishing to reduce immigration still further and to discriminate against southeastern Europeans, proposed that the 1890 Census be adopted as the basis of the quotas rather than the 1910 one employed in the 1921 law, because the 1890 Census would permit much smaller numbers to come in from southern and eastern Europe.

Those favoring the 1910 or even the 1920 Census maintained that the perfectly natural thing to do in any computation is to consult the latest available facts and not some arbitrarily selected set of statistics. They also argued that there was no logical reason why those enumerated in the 1890 Census, most of whom were dead, should be consulted in

making computations for legislation in the year of
our Lord 1924. They further objected to the adoption of the 1890 Census on the grounds that its
selection would mean going out of the way to insult
many peoples of Europe and Asia by deliberately
discriminating against them. Why the 1890 Census,
they continued, why not go the whole way? Why
not adopt the 1790 Census which enumerated almost
entirely people whom you desire? Why not declare
frankly and openly to all men that none other need
apply than citizens, let us say, of the English speaking nations, and be done with it?

The restrictionists, on the other hand, insisted
that the "racial" stock and national unity must be
preserved, and that this could be achieved best by
the adoption of the Census of 1890, which would keep
out as many southeastern Europeans as possible. As
time went on the argument was advanced that in
computing the number of those to be admitted the
native born as well as the foreign born should also
be counted. In the form in which the bill finally
became law the 1890 Census was adopted to apply
until June 30, 1927 and the "national origin" basis
of computation to become operative after that date.
Under this last provision the numerical limit was
arbitrarily set at 150,000 and "the annual quota of
any nationality shall be a number which bears the
same ratio to 150,000 as the number of inhabitants
in continental United States in 1920 . . . whose

origin or ancestry is attributable to such geographical area," except that persons born or tracing their
ancestry to "contiguous territory", "aliens ineligible
to citizenship and their descendants, the descendant
of slave immigrants, or the descendants of American
aborigines", shall not be counted in computing
quotas.[1]

The discussion in both Houses of Congress was
heated to the extreme, indicating how deeply the
nation's representatives were feeling on the matter,
and how high emotions can run on racial and national
issues. Charts, graphs, maps of all shades, color
and size were presented. The debates were long and
passionate. Personal thrusts and counterthrusts
were frequently indulged in even though the record
of many of them were deleted from the Congressional
Record. One large Senator from Alabama held the
Senate more than once wrapped with attention and
fear as he dramatized the Italian coming into
America and with stealthy steps—imitated by the
Senator on the floor—steals behind and . . . .
stabs! the American youth.

The principal supporters in the initial stages were
representatives of the South and the Far West,
while the legislators from New York and Chicago
steadily fought the pending measure. But the opposition was at all times ineffectual, and the bill passed

[1] On March 3, 1927, Congress postponed the application of
this provision until June 30, 1928.

both houses with large majorities—the House 308 to 58 and the Senate 69 to 9,—and by the signature of President Coolidge it became law on May 26, 1924, and effective on July 1, 1924.

To judge the temper into which the country had been worked up during the discussion of immigration legislation and to understand what some of the influences backing the movement were, it is worth noting that during the time that the dispute was at its highest, one dark night, on the hill across the Potomac and overlooking the Capitol there appeared a huge flaming cross, covering acres of ground, and reported by the Washington papers as having consisted of some 5,000 Klan members, bearing torches of pitch and tar.

The new law was hailed by at least one person who for years had been associated with the anti-alien movement (*Foreign Affairs*, September 1924), as the most constructive law enacted in a period of thirty years, "a second Declaration of Independence", "an epoch-making" event, marking a "turning point in American civilization", while its creators and promoters were pronounced the saviors of their country. The analysis of the law contained in the next chapter throws some light upon these claims.

CHAPTER VII

AMERICA ALL BUT CLOSED—1924

We should receive all with impartiality. It should
be our pride to exhibit an example of one nation, at
least, destitute of national antipathies, and exercising,
not merely the overt acts of hospitality, but those
more rare and noble courtesies which spring from
liberality of opinion. What have we to do with
national prejudices? They are the inveterate diseases
of old countries, contracted in rude and ignorant
ages, when nations knew but little of each other, and
looked beyond their own boundaries with distrust and
hostility. We, on the contrary, have sprung into
national existence in an enlightened and philosophic
age, . . . and we forego the advantages of our birth,
if we do not shake off the national prejudices, as
we would the local superstitions, of the old world.
                                    —*Washington Irving.*

I

THE ideal set forth in these words of Washington
Irving, one of the noblest ever placed before a nation,
was followed in the main for a century of national
life and contributed in no small measure to making
the United States a veritable *New World;* and there
are those who maintain that constructive statesman-
ship could still pursue that ideal without necessarily
jeopardizing America's interests. Americans who
take this position, among whom the writer includes

himself, do not object to restriction. They only would wish that in this as in all relations with other peoples we might base our policy and actions upon reason rather than prejudice; that the United States might be the one nation to strive to keep above national antipathies or alien persecutions or at least one people who would not permit degrading race hatreds to take root and become fixed in national legislation.

How far the Immigration Act of 1924 embodies the principles just mentioned an examination of the law itself will best reveal. In general the 1924 law deviates from previous legislation in four major respects: (1) it greatly reduces the number of aliens admissible, (2) it provides for preliminary "examination" and certification abroad, (3) it takes an initial step toward positive selection and (4) it greatly extends the principle of selection-by-rejection by definitely and completely excluding certain races and by indirectly reducing the number admissible from other "racial" groups.

The number admissible is the lowest minimum thus far adopted in the history of immigration to the United States—about 165,000 a year under the quotas, until June 30, 1927 [1] and after that 150,000

[1] Congress on March 3, 1927, postponed the application of this provision until June 30, 1928.

a year. This reduction was effected by two principal
changes in the quota law of 1921: by lessening the
percentage from 3 to 2 and by shifting the quota
basis from 1910, when 9,249,000 foreign born persons were in the United States, to the 1890 Census,
which enumerated 8,000,000 foreign born residents.
The figure of 150,000, which was to apply after
1927, was arbitrarily set and the distribution of
quotas to be made on the basis of "national origin"
which will take into account both the foreign born
and the native born population.

In addition, the 1924 law makes further reductions
by cutting down the exempt classes or making certain safeguards. Thus, for example, while the law
of 1921 permitted persons who had resided in "contiguous territory" for five years, immediately preceding, to enter the United States irrespective of
quotas, the 1924 law exempts only persons *born*
within such territory.

Again, under the former law, actors, artists, lecturers, singers, nurses, persons belonging to the
recognized professions and domestic servants were
permitted to enter after the quotas were exhausted.
Under the 1924 law, on the other hand, they are
allowed to enter only as quota immigrants. Moreover, under the new law, ministers, teachers and students are required to *offer proof* of such a nature as
to practically prohibit their coming—a point which
will be treated in a subsequent paragraph. Obvi-

ously these and other provisions, while aiming to make safeguards, do nevertheless indirectly tend to reduce total immigration.

Whether the 1924 law will actually reduce numbers is too early to determine at this writing, for the simple reason that, as we have seen in the case of the 1921 law, it takes some time before the full effect of the law can be measured. Several provisions of the present law may prevent a substantial and permanent dimunition. In the first place, "contiguous" countries, Canada, Newfoundland, Mexico, Cuba, Haiti, the Canal Zone, the Dominican Republic and the independent countries of Central and South America, are all exempt from the quota provisions. This leaves free channels of considerable size through which thousands of aliens will undoubtedly continue to enter the United States.

It is not at all impossible, moreover, that immigration from exempted territory will make an even greater permanent addition to the labor forces of this country than an equal number of Europeans would make, because immigrants from contiguous nations do not return to their countries in the same proportion as those from Europe. For example, during the years 1917-23, inclusive, total immigration from Canada and Mexico was 754,845, while the number of those returning to these two countries

was only 142,852, leaving a total net immigration
from these nations of 611,993. European immigrants, on the other hand, numbered 1,611,739 during this period, but emigrants numbered 851,029,
thus leaving a net increase from European sources
of but 760,710, or only 148,717 more than from
Canada and Mexico alone. While these data are
not altogether conclusive on account of the fact that
they cover the war and early postwar situation, they
do suggest that when the full effects of the 1924
immigration law are measured it may possibly be
found that it makes a larger permanent addition to
the labor population of the United States than former laws.

The reductions intended by the 1924 law, furthermore, have been greatly offset in actuality, though
not in statistical tables, by increased surreptitious
entries. These have steadily gained as the immigration laws have become more restrictive, as we have
already seen. What occurred in the case of seamen
who increased from 5,879 in 1922 to 23,194 in 1923,
and 34,679 in 1924 is indicative of what may occur
in the case of general illegal immigration.

In the matter of surreptitious entries it needs to
be constantly borne in mind that we are dealing with
basic human forces which impel men on. So long as
an individual considers his coming into the United
States or any other country a matter of life and
death, so long, reprehensible as it may be, will he

take great chances to effect that entrance. And in proportion as it becomes more difficult to gain the coveted prize, the greater the hazards he will run to gain it.

II

In providing for *preliminary inquiry* and *certification* abroad, the Immigration Act of 1924 contributes the first broadly constructive principle to be incorporated in our immigration law. It is interesting to note in this connection that the system of examination and certification in the countries of origin had been advocated for more than sixty years before 1924.[1] And this in turn illustrates the fact often observed that legislation almost invariably lags far behind progressive thinking and sometimes even behind general public opinion.

Contrary to general belief, however, the 1924 law *does not* provide for an *examination* abroad, but only for a *preliminary inquiry* to discover whether the intending emigrants can meet the requirements of the United States immigration law. It requires the emigrant to fill out and present in person, in duplicate form, a prescribed blank calling for complete descriptive information regarding himself

[1] Cf. *Charities and Corrections,* 1887, 195-197, 214; *Forum,* 1887, 540; 50th. Congress, *House Report,* Miscellaneous Documents No. 572, pt. 2: 1123; *Forum,* 1889-1890, 438-440; 51st. Congress, *House Report,* No. 3472, 149; *Congressional Record,* March 16, 1896, 2817-2820; *Annual Report of the Commissioner General of Immigration,* 1900, 40-41.

and his family. He has to certify that he is able to "speak, read and write", that he has not been an inmate of an almshouse, a prison, and that neither he nor either of his parents has been a patient in an institution for the care of the insane. The prospective emigrant is also required to furnish two photographs and birth certificates, two copies of his "dossier", prison and military record, if any, and "of all other available records" concerning himself and his family which may be in the possession of the government to which he owes allegiance.

If the United States Consular Officer is satisfied that the alien can meet the requirements of the immigration law, upon payment of $10.00 per person, he issues a visa. The visa remains valid for four months from the date of issuance. Before that time has expired the migrant must have actually departed from his country and proceeded on a continuous voyage to the United States or else he must secure another visa. Visas are required of all immigrants, quota and non-quota alike. Courts have ruled, however, that an alien who can establish previous residence in the United States is admissible after absence even though he does not have a visa or a permit to reënter.

The preliminary inquiry and the possession of an unexpired visa do not free the immigrant from examination at the port of arrival nor do they in any way guarantee his admission, since he is still subject to the usual examinations. Although this system leaves the possibility of some being rejected after arrival, the experience of the last three years shows that the number of persons possessing visas who are rejected is almost negligible.

As indicative of the temper of our time it is worthy of special note that the 1924 immigration law, while making generous exemptions in favor of persons engaged in commerce or international trade, places great difficulties in the way of ministers, teachers and students, and even more severe obstacles in the way of members of the families of both aliens and naturalized citizens.

The law practically deprives teachers and ministers the privilege of migrating to the United States. The law specifies that ministers and teachers must not only submit evidence confirming their status, but must also *definitely prove* that they are to continue in their professions after arrival. By the very nature of the case these proofs can seldom be procured before entering this country, and therefore the law makes it almost impossible for a professor or minister to come to the United States to start life anew, except as a temporary visitor.

Upon students the law places even more onerous burdens. Aside from meeting all the other requirements the student must designate the exact university or college to which he intends to go in the United States before he has been in this country or has had opportunity to know its educational institutions. The institution must be on the approved list of the

Secretary of Labor. The student, moreover, must specify the precise course he is to pursue, and submit conclusive evidence that he has "sufficient funds to defray all expenses during his stay in the United States or that payment thereof is properly secured and that he will be able to devote his time solely to study." The executive requirements further state that if admitted to the United States the student "who engages in any business or occupation for profit; or who labors for hire shall be deemed to have abandoned his status as an immigrant student and shall on the warrant of the Secretary of Labor be taken into custody and deported."

It would seem as if these requirements unnecessarily take away a great privilege from students of other lands who might wish to come to the United States to acquire an education. In the past one of the best contributions this country has made has been that it has offered impecunious young foreigners an opportunity to secure an education; and the number who have availed themselves of this privilege and have worked their way through schools and colleges must be large. The present law takes this privilege away, except that students as well as teachers and ministers may come under the quotas, which as we have seen are exceedingly small. If the provisions of the 1924 law continue in force it may be that in the future those who wish to gain an education which they cannot secure in their own countries must seek some other country.

The requirements made of immigrants who may wish to bring their relatives to the United States are even more onerous. In order to bring his wife and children under eighteen years of age to this country, as non-quota immigrants, a naturalized United States citizen must follow a course entailing considerable expense and countless delays. He is required to file with the Commissioner General of Immigration a petition giving his name and address, numerous facts relative to his naturalization, the name and address of his employer, or his place of business, the degree of relationship of the person or persons whom he intends to bring to this country, the names of *all places* where these persons have resided and a declaration that he is able to support them. The petition, made under oath, must be supported by "documentary evidence", accompanied by a statement of two or more "responsible" citizens of the United States, who have known the petitioner personally for at least one year and vouch for the statements made in the petition. Then the petition goes to the Commissioner General of Immigration in Washington. The Commissioner then secures the approval of the Secretary of Labor. If the petition is granted the information is transmitted to the Secretary of State, who then notifies the United States consular officer abroad *by mail*—unless the petitioner wishes to pay for cable charges—and the consular officer informs the relative that he or she is entitled to *make application* for a non-quota immigration visa.

The practical difficulties alone which this circuitous system creates are many and varied. Many foreign born persons reside at considerable distance from immigration bureau centers and from other sources of information. Even if they reside close at hand the securing of information, the proper filling out and transmitting of petitions, the proper transmitting of information to the relatives abroad, involve expense, loss of work and great suspense. Even under the most favorable conditions there is no escape from an endless chain of applications and reapplications, correspondence and painful waiting, delays and counter delays and unending anxiety. Of course, wives and children of citizens may come as quota immigrants; but the quotas for most countries are now so small that little relief can come from this source.

These difficulties apply even more in the case of aliens already in this country. For a time, in 1924 and 1925, a peculiar deadlock between the immigration law and the practice of many courts in granting citizenship made it impossible for an alien to secure his citizenship because his family was not in this country or to bring his family because he was not a citizen. An alien established in this country, who for some reason had not become a citizen, wishing to bring his family to this country was told by immigration officers: "You cannot bring your wife and children as non-quota immigrants because you are not a citizen." "Very well," responded the man, "I have always intended to become a citizen and have only been prevented from doing so because of my having moved about in search of work until I came to this city where I established myself in business. I will therefore make application for citizenship." In many courts, however, the alien met with the reply: "This Court cannot grant you citizenship because you do not have your family in this country." So he could not bring his family over because he was not a citizen and he could not become a citizen because his family was not in this country. Or supposing the Court to which he applies does entertain his declaration or his petition for citizenship. Still he has from two to five years to wait. Of course he can attempt to bring his relatives as quota immigrants. But the quotas are so small under the present law for most countries that in any event he is utterly helpless and has nothing but endless waiting before him.

It is altogether probable that these complications developed accidentally, but if they were deliberately created by the fertile brain of some legislator, they may be considered one of the most perfidious schemes ever devised by the brain of man to torture and injure his fellowmen. And this is especially true when it is remembered that most immigrants are simple-

minded people, much devoted and affectionate in
their family life. The complications and hardships
seem to have been so severe that the matter came to
the attention of President Coolidge, who referred to
them both in his messages of 1924 and 1925. In the
former he said: "I should like to see the administrative features of this [immigration] law rendered a
little more humane for the purpose of permitting
those already here a greater latitude in securing
admission of members of their families."

Two general criticisms are directed to the visa
system. First, it is believed that the preliminary
inquiry abroad is at best perfunctory. The consular
officer can not do more than certify to the correct-
ness of an official of a given country. He cannot
inquire into the statements that are set forth in the
papers which form the major part of the "examination"; nor can he do other than certify a foreign
official's signature. This objection, however, applies
more to the type of "examination" than to the visa
system as such, and to a discussion of this point we
shall return later.

Some critics also believe that the visa system
would open a wide avenue for corruption by placing
too great authority in the hands of one man. Senator Copeland of New York said in the Senate: "Is
there going to be any chance for log rolling or cor-

ruption of any sort in the issuance of these certificates? Does it not place undue power in the hands of a consul in some obscure part of the earth, that he may use preference, perhaps immoral preference, in the issuance of these certificates?" The 1924 law, however, has been in operation now for nearly three years. Under these provisions immigration "technical advisers" are functioning in some twenty United States consulates and no serious abuses of this sort have developed.

The visa system as a whole, however, provides a vast improvement upon that formerly in practice. Under it the confusion and tragedies attendant upon the law of 1921 are eliminated. The centralization of information already being carried out in Europe and the careful handling of visas by the consular agents has so worked out that very few immigrants now leave their country of origin or any country without definite assurance that they are clearly within the quota and the admissible classes and that barring extraordinary developments they will be admitted to the United States.

III

It was previously stated that the Immigration Act of 1924 takes an initial step toward *positive selection*. This is done principally in Section 6, which provides for preferences within the quotas. That section states that in granting visas combined preference shall be given, to the extent of fifty per cent of the monthly or annual quota, to fathers and mothers, wives and unmarried children under twenty-one years of age of American citizens, *and* to persons "skilled in agriculture."

In giving preference within quotas to agriculturists—who by executive orders are defined as farmers and farm laborers who are skilled in planting, cultivating and harvesting of crops and persons skilled in forestry, horticulture and animal husbandry—the legislators undoubtedly intended to select, by occupation, those whom they considered were needed in the further development of this country. This particular provision was included in deference to the wishes of the South, particularly North Carolina. Although it is questionable whether at present the country is actually in need of agriculturists, yet this first appearance in immigration legislation of the principle of selection by occupation is to be commended and is one which might well be extended to apply to all immigrants alike.

The combined preference given to relatives and farmers, however, like the visa provisions of the law, is liable to work injury to the family unit and should be so improved as to eliminate this possibility. The law states that preference shall not be given to relatives over agriculturists, but fails to state that agriculturists shall not be preferred above relatives. In this lies the possibility of giving agriculturists a preference and of putting the economic needs of the country above its social well-being. Moreover, relatives, as already pointed out, are obliged to furnish proofs of relationship based upon documents emanating in the United States and therefore not easily procurable; agriculturists, on the other hand, are called upon to furnish proofs easily available in their parent countries, and thereby have a tremendous advantage over relatives.

IV

By far the most far-reaching aspect of the new law is the qualitative provision implied in the distribution of quotas by "races" or peoples. These provisions, broadly speaking, (1) completely exclude the Asiatics and certain other non-white "races" and (2) practically exclude certain subdivisions of the Caucasian "race"; that is, all the peoples of southern and eastern Europe.

The annual quota of any nationality, states the law, shall be two per centum of the number of foreign-born individuals of such a nationality resident in Continental United States as determined by the United States Census of 1890, but the minimum quota of any nationality shall be 100. The Secretary of State, the Secretary of Commerce and the Secretary of Labor are authorized to determine the quotas and to report annually to the President, who shall proclaim and make known the quotas so reported.

The quotas as proclaimed originally follow:

ANNUAL QUOTAS, UNDER THE IMMIGRATION ACT OF 1924

Country or Area of Birth	Annual Quota	Country or Area of Birth	Annual Quota
*Afghanistan	100	Monaco	100
Albania	100	Morocco	100
Andorrs	100	*Muscat (Oman)	100
Arabian peninsula	100	Nauru (British)	100
Armenia	124	*Nepal	100
Australia	121	†Netherlands	1,648
Austria	785	New Zealand	100
†Belgium	512	*New Guinea	100
*Bhutan	100	†Norway	6,453
Bulgaria	100	Palestine	100
Cameroon (British)	100	Persia	100
Cameroon (French)	100	Poland	5,982
*China	100	†Portugal	503
Czechoslovakia	3,073	Ruandia and Urundi.	100
Danzig	228	Rumania	603
†Denmark	2,789	Russia, European and	
Egypt	100	Asiatic	2,248
Esthonia	124	Samoa, Western	100
Ethiopia (Abyssinia).	100	San Marino	100
Finland	471	*Siam	100
†France	3,954	South Africa	100
Germany	51,227	South West Africa	100
†Great Britain and		†Spain	131
Northern Ireland	34,007	Sweden	9,561
Greece	100	Switzerland	2,081
Hungary	473	Syria and The Leb-	
Iceland	100	anon	100
*India	100	Tanganyika	100
Iraq (Mesopotamia)	100	Togoland (British)	100
Irish Free State	28,567	Togoland (French)	100
†Italy	3,845	Turkey	100
*Japan	100	*Yap and other Pacific	
Latvia	142	Islands	100
Liberia	100	Yugoslavia	671
Liechtenstein	100		
Lithuania	344	Total	164,667
Luxemburg	100		

* Quotas for the countries marked by the asterisk are intended only for persons born within those countries, who belong to the races eligible to citizenship in the United States. For example: a person born in India of English parentage may be admitted, but a Hindu may not.—The Author.

† Including colonies, dependencies, or protectorates of this country.

These 1924 quotas reduce the 1921 quotas for all
the countries subject to the quota regulation. These
reductions, however, vary greatly: greatest in the
case of southern and eastern Europe and least in
that of the northern and western countries of
Europe. But in the case of no country or region of
birth is the quota less than 100. This provision is
somewhat misleading. It does not mean that 100
of any "race" may enter, but only 100 of a "race"
not excluded by other provisions of the law. For
instance, 100 persons born in China of Caucasian
"race" may come from that country but not a 100
Chinese.

A comparison of the 1921 and the 1924 quotas
brought out in the compilation [1] on page 149 makes
clear what peoples are given preference.

The changes indicated in the foregoing table are
the result of a movement which has been going on
for a number of years in the United States. As early
as March 16, 1896, Senator Lodge, one of the chief
proponents of this movement, urged Congress to
enact a law which would reduce immigration from
southern and southeastern Europe, saying that a
continued immigration from that source involved
"nothing less than the possibility of a great and
perilous change in the very fabric of our race."

This underlying motive, rather than economic
necessity, appears to have been the primary moving

[1] Commissioner General of Immigration, *Report,* 1924, p. 27.

Country or Region of Birth	Act of 1921	Act of 1924	Country or Region of Birth	Act of 1921	Act of 1924
Albania	288	100	Luxemburg ...	92	100
Armenia (Rus-			Netherlands ...	3,607	1,648
sia)	230	124	Norway	12,202	6,453
Austria	7,342	785	Poland	30,977	5,982
Belgium	1,563	512	Portugal	2,465	503
Bulgaria	302	100	Roumania	7,419	603
Czechoslovakia .	14,357	3,073	Russia	24,405	2,248
Danzig	301	228	Spain	912	131
Denmark	5,619	2,789	Sweden	20,042	9,561
Esthonia	1,348	124	Switzerland ...	3,752	2,081
Finland	3,921	471	Yugoslavia	6,426	671
France	5,729	3,954	Palestine	57	100
Germany	67,607	51,227	Syria	882	100
Great Britain,			Turkey	2,654	100
Ireland	77,342	34,007	Australia	279	121
Greece	3,063	100	New Zealand		
Hungary	5,747	473	and Pacific		
Iceland	75	100	Islands	80	100
†Irish Free State	..	28,567	All others	492	3,100
Italy	42,057	3,845			
Latvia	1,540	142	Total	357,803	164,667
Lithuania	2,629	344			

† Included in Great Britain and Ireland, under Act of 1921.

force leading to "race" discrimination. Representative Albert Johnson of Washington, in fact, so stated in a signed article in *The Nation's Business* (July 1923): "the new measure thus aims to change the character of our future immigration by cutting down the number of aliens who can come from southern and eastern Europe. In other words, it is clearly recognized that, on the whole, northern and western Europe furnish the best material for citizenship." And Commissioner General of Immigration W.

W. Husband, writing in *Journal of Commerce*
(January 15, 1924), stated that "the purpose of
the percentage law is clearly to leave the way wide
open for all northern and western Europeans who
may desire to come but to close the doors as much
as possible to those coming from southern and eastern Europe."

The total exclusion of Asiatics, Hindus et cetera
is in reality only the extension of this same general
movement. The Chinese were debarred in 1882; the
Japanese were excluded for all practical purposes
by the so-called "gentlemen's agreement" of 1907.
In 1917 the "barred zone" was created by which the
natives of all China and Afghanistan, of India, Siam
and the East Indies were prohibited from entering
the United States. The law of 1924, however, does
make the important departure of extending the principle of rejection to given countries or regions of
birth occupied by certain subdivisions of the Caucasian "race".

These two aspects of the law; namely, (1) the
singling out of southern and southeastern European
"racial" and national elements for limited rejection
and (2) the complete exclusion of the Japanese—
discussed at length in the next chapter—have already
engendered considerable ill-feeling. The fullest significance of this act cannot be understood at present,
nor the possible consequences foretold.

The large quota allowed to Ireland and the per-

mitting of Mexicans to enter without reference to
quota has caused considerable comment. It is at
best questionable whether these people can contribute
more to the total well-being of the nation than equal
numbers of southern and southeastern Europeans.
In addition the 1924 law clearly aims to put the
West and Southwest on a preferential basis. Speaking on this point, Representative Sabath of Illinois
on April 5, 1924, remarked on the floor of the House:
"Unfortunately for the country this House has
selected an Immigration Committee—I do not know
whether deliberately or only by chance—made up of
four members from the Pacific coast and six from
the South. . . . Last year from Canada alone we
had 117,011 immigrants in addition to a large number of Mexicans, but no criticism has been made.
. . . This committee, this great committee, that has
investigated this question so thoroughly, could not
find a way to embody a provision in the bill that
would place Mexico and Canada in the same position
in which they are placing other countries." Numerous persons in all parts of the United States are
advocating the extension of the quota system to
countries in the Western Hemisphere. Commissioner
General of Immigration, Harry E. Hull, said on
October 11, 1926: "The unfairness of permitting
unlimited numbers, figuratively, to come in through
practically an open door, as they may now, is
apparent."

V

At this writing the Immigration Act of 1924 has been in operation nearly three years. Complete statistics are available for the years 1925, 1926 and for the first six months of 1927,[1] and therefore we can measure some of the general effects. During the first year, 1925, 294,314 immigrants were admitted; in 1926, 304,488 and in the six months, July 1 to December 31, 1926, 175,955. Departures amounted to 92,728 for 1925; 76,992 for 1926 and 42,779 for the period of July 1 to December 31, 1926 inclusive. This left a net immigration of 201,586 for 1925; 227,496 for 1926 and 133,176 for the six months specified.

The effect the law is having on actually giving preference to northern and western over southern and eastern Europeans may be illustrated by the figures for 1925. Of the immigrants admitted in 1925, 75.6 per cent belonged to the northern and western European group. This represented a substantial increase over the proportion of 55.7 per cent admitted from those peoples in 1924 and of 25.7 per cent in 1921. The peoples of southern and eastern Europe and Turkey in 1925 contributed 10.8 per cent as compared with 27.0 during 1924 and 66.7 per cent in 1921. Mexicans contributed in 1925

[1] Throughout designated years are fiscal years, ending June 30th.

about 11 per cent, a slight decrease from the 12.4 per cent of 1923-24, although their actual numbers fell from 87,648 to 32,278. The number of English speaking immigrants—English, Irish, Scotch and Welsh—amounted to 121,911, or more than one-half of the net immigration, increasing from 28.3 of the total immigration in 1924 to 41.4 per cent for 1925.

Almost exactly one-half of the immigrants admitted in 1925 or 145,971 were quota immigrants, the remainder had non-quota status. In 1925 Germany, Sweden, Great Britain and the Irish Free State did not fill their quota by substantial margins. Czechoslovakia had a balance of 107, Jugoslavia of 103, Hungary 106, and Italy 1,149. At no time since 1922 have Great Britain, Germany and the Scandinavian countries reached the quotas assigned to them. This situation may indicate that Europe has caught the spirit of the recent United States immigration legislation and that even groups with preferential status are turning elsewhere.

In addition considerable numbers are leaving this country. During 1925, 92,728 aliens left the United States, by far the larger proportion belonging to national groups discriminated against. In that year more Bulgarians, Czechoslovaks, Greeks, Hungarians, Italians, Lithuanians, Portuguese, Roumanians, Spaniards, Turks, Armenians, Chinese, Japanese, Cubans and other West Indians, Australians and

New Zealanders left this country than came in; 6,574 Greeks left while only 826 were admitted; 27,151 Italians departed, 6,203 arrived; 3,600 Portuguese emigrated from this country, 619 came in; 3,982 Spaniards left and only 275 entered; 3,412 Chinese departed and 1,927 came in; 1,212 Japanese left, 723 arrived.

The majority of those departing from this country belong to the older and cultured national groups. It appears that many foreign born residents of this country have been seriously affected, not so much by restriction, as by the bitterness engendered by the race discrimination movement. Americans, both native and foreign born who believe that a nation should build itself up by amity, by considerateness and courtesy rather than by might and categorical discrimination, tend to take a sober view of the matter. The hope is entertained in many quarters that in time the situation may be altered and possible grave consequences be avoided. For it is a well established principle that nations which inflict wounds tend soon to forget, whereas the wounded bear the marks upon their bodies and souls and pass them on to the coming generations. That creates sharp cleavages between nations. And this applies to no people so much as to the Japanese, the story of whose exclusion we shall now endeavor to review.

CHAPTER VIII

"GRAVE CONSEQUENCES"

Resolved, etc., that the people of the United States
assert as a fundamental principle that the rights of
its citizens shall not be impaired at home or abroad
because of race or religion; that the Government of
the United States concludes its treaties for the equal
protection of all classes of its citizens, without
regard to race or religion; that the Government of
the United States will not be a party to any treaty
which discriminates, or which by one of the parties
thereto is so construed as to discriminate, between
American citizens on the ground of race or religion.
—*House Joint Resolutoin* 166, Dec. 13, 1911.

I

PERHAPS no more dramatic and important moment
has ever occurred in the history of immigration than
that occurring in the United States Senate on
the afternoon of April 14, 1924. The shrill bells
sounded three times throughout the capitol build-
ings—a warning rarely heard at the United
States Capitol. The large red light flashed above
the side door of the Senate floor. The newspaper
men demurely vacated their stalls above the President of the Senate's desk. Clerks and secretaries

hastily closed their recording books. Page boys, half amused and half bewildered, filed out one by one casting backward glances. The beedles, with magisterial air, shooed the public from the galleries. The Sergeant-at-Arms assumed control of the doors . . . and . . . the United States Senate, on motion of Senator Lodge, passed into executive session.

Fifty minutes later the doors were thrown open. Junior Senator Shortridge of California was speaking: "It is time for action rather than for speech," he was saying, ". . . As to our power and our duty, we must be sure of both before taking action. . . . We should act along the line suggested . . .; for social and racial reasons we should so act. . . . It is our duty first and always so to act without asking for or getting the consent of any other nation, be that nation mighty or feeble, civilized or barbarous, great on land or great on sea . . . We are asking here and now, speaking as a Nation, to adopt an immigration policy which shall run hand in hand, alongside of, and in harmony with our national policy as to naturalization or citizenship. Who comes forward here now to object to this Nation exercising its universally acknowledged sovereign right and power? Who is it that intrudes into our councils? Who is it that insolently and impertinently demands that we abdicate, that we surrender our sovereignty; that, indeed, we surrender our very independence of action as an independent Nation? Who is it that does this

thing? The Senate knows; the country knows!"
(*Congressional Record*, April 14, 1924.)

II

In order to understand how important was the
question the Senate was discussing and what led one
of its members to make the speech from which we
have cited it will be necessary to trace step by step
the events which led up to it.

It was about the middle of the last century, 1853
to be precise, that Commodore Perry, in the name of
the United States, virtually forced Japan to open its
doors to the outside world. For two centuries or
more the Japanese people had been in seclusion, had
little or no intercourse with other nations and by
the law of the land were commanded to remain at
home. The visit of Perry's Black Ships, however,
began to send the Japanese abroad, and although
their Government did not grant its subjects permission to emigrate until 1885, a few came to America
before that time. In 1870 there were 55 Japanese in
this country and in 1880 but 148. In the two
decades following they began to come in appreciable
numbers, and in 1900 over 12,000 Japanese entered
the United States.

It was during that year that "the yellow peril"
scare, which previously had applied to the Chinese,
now was directed to the Japanese. Objections partly
social but more economic were raised by portions of

California's population to their coming. The thrifty and hard working Japanese were taking a conspicuous and successful part in San Francisco's petty business, particularly in the restaurant trade. This aroused the ire of competitors who created and crystallized anti-Japanese sentiment.

The first organized demand for the exclusion of the Japanese was formulated during that same year. A mass meeting was held in San Francisco on May 7, 1900 at which speeches were made, patriotic songs sung and a resolution adopted. The resolution called upon Congress to reënact the Chinese exclusion law of 1882 and also to pass a law prohibiting the entrance of all classes of Japanese except members of the diplomatic staff. Subsequently messages from the Governor's office and resolutions from the State Legislature called upon Congress to extend the Chinese exclusion law to other Asiatics. However, little or no interest was taken in the matter by the people at large in California (Millis: *The Japanese Problem in the United States*), until, in 1905 the *San Francisco Chronicle* took up the cudgel and conducted a vigorous campaign against the Japanese. The large numbers of Japanese coming to the mainland from Honolulu in the spring of 1905 greatly swelled the number of those coming directly from Japan and gave the appearance of a veritable flood. The Asiatic Exclusion League was organized in May,

1905, "this being, in a sense, ready made of the trade unions which had always been in the thick of the fight against Chinese immigration." Feeling ran so high "that an appeal to the right of revolution would be a possibility if the desires of the residents were not regarded." (Millis.)

III

On April 18, 1906 the Portola Fault gave way and the city of San Francisco, "the smelting-pot of the races" as Stevenson was wont to call her, lay in a mass of ruins and flames, its people shelterless and bewildered.

Common suffering, which usually binds peoples in mutual sympathy and helpfulness, in this case produced far different results. Although Japan, through the Japanese Red Cross, contributed more money to the relief of the San Francisco sufferers than all the other foreign nations put together, so great was the hold that prejudice had gained, that agitators seized upon this time to deal the Japanese a blow!

The result was the now famous "separate school order." The San Francisco school authorities, claiming that a scarcity of accommodation made it necessary, ordered the ninety-three Japanese children, who before the fire were in the public schools, to attend the so-called Oriental school, which was "located in the center of the city, far removed from the homes of most of the pupils and under the circumstances almost inaccessible." (Millis.)

The Japanese people understood the real significance of the "separate school order." They objected. Their children refused to obey. The Japanese Consulate protested. And the matter assumed national and international importance. From the National Capitol President Roosevelt at once sent an investigator to California. Later, in a special communication to Congress, he upheld the Japanese children and stated that the Federal Government had directed that a suit be brought to test the constitutionality of the action. In his annual message to Congress of December 3, 1906, the President said: "To shut them out of the public schools is a wicked absurdity."

American public opinion was clearly with the President, as the literature of the times indicates. School authorities throughout the nation condemned the action of the San Francisco Board; also public officials, business men, writers did the same. In every quarter regrets were voiced that at the very moment when East and West were coming into closer relationships such an act should have been thought necessary. It would be "both folly and a crime" said the *Outlook* editorially, "to alienate the great and powerful nations. . . ."

The California Legislature, however, proceeded to

take steps to make the action of the local board constitutional. The Federal Government once more
intervened, objecting not so much to the exclusion of
the Japanese as to the manner in which a small seg-
ment of the people of one state were dealing with a
situation which was clearly national and international in scope. The controversy led to a series of
conferences between the United States Department
of State and the Japanese Embassy, which resulted
in the far-famed "gentlemen's agreement," concluded
in 1907 by Secretary of State Root and Japanese
Ambassador Takahira.

Unfortunately *secret diplomacy* kept the "gentlemen's agreement" buried in the archives of the State
Department, in the correspondence carried on during
a period of over a year. Thus one more votive offering was made to the god of misunderstanding
between peoples. For had the American public and
even the people of California as a whole known
what the contents and the spirit of the "agreement"
were, it might have prevented the unpleasant developments which followed.

The only knowledge we have of the "gentlemen's
agreement" to this day is based upon a statement
appearing in the Report of the Commissioner General of Immigration for 1908, which in part reads
as follows: "This understanding contemplates that
the Japanese Government shall issue passports to
continental United States only to such of its subjects

as are non-laborers or are laborers who, in coming to the continent, seek to resume a formerly acquired domicile, to join a parent, wife or children residing there, or to assume active control of an already possessed interest in a farming enterprise in this country. . . ."

IV

The "gentlemen's agreement" seemed, therefore, to promise a solution of the problem, since it aimed to stop the immigration of Japanese laborers and small enterprisers, and thus eliminate the basic causes of friction.

Statements regarding the extent to which the "gentlemen's agreement" produced an adequate solution of the Japanese immigration problem differ with the sources from which they come. From the day of its adoption to the enactment of the 1924 Immigration Law a heated controversy went on. Statistics were compiled and marshalled on each side and the same figures were made to tell widely divergent tales.

United States official statistics, primarily taken from the Reports of the Commissioner General of Immigration, tell the following story: During the decade immediately *preceding* the adoption of the "agreement" the immigration of Japanese into this country had been increasing at a rapid rate—Japanese immigrant aliens were arriving at the rate of over 14,000 a year, reaching the high mark of 30,824 in the fiscal year 1907.[1]

JAPANESE IMMIGRANT ALIENS, 1899-1907 [2]

Fiscal year ending June 30th		Fiscal year ending June 30th	
1899	3,395	1904	14,382
1900	12,628	1905	11,021
1901	5,249	1906	14,243
1902	14,455	1907	30,824
1903	20,041		

During the years immediately *following* the adoption of the "gentlemen's agreement" Japanese immigration materially decreased. For the years 1908-14 it averaged 7,211 or about one-half of that of the previous period. During these years also the outward flow of Japanese from this country was large, especially in the first years after the adoption of the "agreement" as is seen from the table on page 164; although no figures of emigration are available before 1908 and therefore no comparison can be made in this regard.

From the beginning of the World War to the end of the fiscal year 1924 both immigration and emigration fluctuated considerably. During 1918, 1919 and 1920 Japanese immigration was comparatively large, due, it is thought, to the war movements of

[1] Throughout designated years are fiscal years, ending June 30.

[2] Commissioner General of Immigration, *Report* 1923, p. 117.

JAPANESE IMMIGRANT AND EMIGRANT ALIENS 1908-1914 [1]

JAPANESE IMMIGRANT ALIENS	JAPANESE EMIGRANT ALIENS
Fiscal year ending June 30th	Fiscal year ending June 30th
1908 16,418	1908 5,323
1909 3,275	1909 3,903
1910 2,798	1910 4,377
1911 4,575	1911 3,351
1912 6,172	1912 1,501
1913 8,302	1913 733
1914 8,941	1914 794

the Japanese. But even then the average for this period was 8,365, a little more than half as much as the average for the years preceding the adoption of the "gentlemen's agreement" and only slightly larger than the prewar volume.

JAPANESE IMMIGRANTS AND EMIGRANTS 1915-1924 [2]

Fiscal year ending June 30th				Fiscal year ending June 30th			
Year	Immig.	Emig.	Net	Year	Immig.	Emig.	Net
1915	 8,609	825	7,784	1920	 9,279	4,238	5,041
1916	 8,711	780	7,921	1921	 7,531	4,352	3,179
1917	 8,925	722	8,203	1922	 6,361	4,353	2,008
1918	10,168	1,558	8,610	1923	 5,652	2,844	2,808
1919	10,056	2,127	7,729	1924	 8,481	2,120	6,361

The inference from these figures would seem to be that the "gentlemen's agreement" had worked quite

[1] Commissioner General of Immigration, op. cit., pp. 117-118, 121.

[2] Commissioner General of Immigration, *Report* 1924, pp. 114, 118.

well in producing the desired end. Unfortunately, however, a complete analysis cannot be made on account of the fact that available statistics do not separate the classes exempted from the "agreement" (members of diplomatic staffs, commercial men, etc.), from Japanese laborers and related groups.

United States Census figures throw supplementary light upon the question. The Census of 1910 enumerated 72,157 Japanese, or 0.1 per cent of the total population. In 1920 they still constituted but 0.1 per cent of the population of the United States, but their number had increased to 111,010. These figures represented an increase of 47,831 or 196.6 per cent between 1900 and 1910 and of 38,853 or 53.8 per cent for the 1910-20 decade; whereas the increase for the total population of the United States was 21.0 per cent in the former period and 14.9 per cent for the latter ten years. Of the 38,853 representing the numerical increase of "Japanese" in the United States during 1910-20, however, nearly two-thirds or 24,901 were born in this country.

These census figures, rather than the record of immigration, furnished the principal basis for the contention that the "gentlemen's agreement" had not solved the problem. Supplementary investigations were made by the State of California which, though locally lending additional proof to this side of the case, cannot be entirely relied upon, as they were made too closely in connection with the controversy to be altogether trustworthy.

V

As a matter of fact it was not figures that supplied the real dynamic to the anti-Japanese movement, but, rather, a number of categorical assertions which, based upon individual observation and opinion and charged with emotion are incapable of proof. Certain elements in California claimed that the Japanese were particularly clannish, that "their racial characteristics, thrift, industry, low standards of living, willingness to work long hours without expensive pleasures, the women laboring as men," gave them unfair advantage in economic competition over American laborers and petty merchants. They further contended that the Japanese sought to control the land situation in California by fair or foul means; that their extraordinary coöperation and solidarity "together with the assistance they received from their Government, made them a political menace"; that "their language, heredity, religion, the law and polity of Japan, all militated against even their sociological [sic] assimilation," and that the Japanese were making a peaceful and conscious penetration by establishing a "government within a government" which would sooner or later dispossess and drive the white race to the wall.

Under the impact of these accusations and by

means of ceaseless efforts, were enacted the anti-alien land laws of California, Washington and Arizona, aimed primarily at the Japanese. In 1913 the California land law declared that the Japanese, being "ineligible to citizenship," would not possess any real property rights that were not granted under the treaty of 1911 between the United States and Japan, except the right to lease land for three years. In 1920 even this right was taken away. In 1923 the Japanese were prohibited from entering into croppage contracts. In November of that year the United States Supreme Court declared that the anti-alien land laws did not violate the treaty of 1911 or the Fourteenth Amendment to the Constitution and held specifically that a State has the right to prohibit croppage contracts.

An attack on a nation-wide scale was also made. In 1922 the matter of the eligibility of Japanese to United States citizenship was taken to the Supreme Court. That body, in keeping with Section 6,129 of the United States Revised Statutes, which restricts naturalization to free white persons and those of African descent, declared the Japanese ineligible to citizenship. Next came, in 1923, two petitions from the California State Legislature asking Congress to enact a law prohibiting all immigrants "ineligible to citizenship", and urging that a constitutional amendment be submitted which should withhold citizenship from persons born in the United States

of parents "ineligible to citizenship." At last, in
November 1923, notice was served on the United
States Secretary of State, "that a measure aiming
to exclude Japanese would be introduced in the coming Congress." (*The International Year Book.*)

VI

In the meantime Japan seems to have done all that
was humanly possible faithfully to observe the "gentlemen's agreement", to satisfy the wishes of the
American people, and even to comply with the excessive demands of those portions of California's population who were pronouncedly anti-Japanese. Cyrus
E. Woods, ex-Ambassador to Japan, in a letter
addressed to the Federal Council of Churches in
quadrennial session in December 1924, said: "Japan
accepted the principle of exclusion in 1908. Since
that date the Japanese Government has been loyally
coöperating with the Government of the United
States in carrying out that policy."

Japan, moreover has at no time thought it expedient that large groups of her people should settle
in the United States. Oscar T. Crosby, former
Assistant Secretary of the Treasury, in *International
War: Its Causes and Cure*, states that "American
public opinion on this particular point has been
erroneously formed. The idea that the Japanese in
California are the forerunners of an overwhelming
swarm of Orientals has been widely fostered. Yet

from any fairly intelligent study of the situation it is found that public opinion in Japan takes quite a contrary view. The rulers of that country do not believe that a vast movement of their people to our shores is either necessary or desirable, but they do believe that no invidious distinctions should be made against their nationals by the laws of the United States, or of any land." (p. 369.)

That this is the spirit which has animated Japan is evident from a number of steps the Japanese Government and people took. In 1913 Japan naturally protested against the California land law on the grounds that the act of that year involved racial discrimination. But in 1920, in order to prevent further misunderstandings, the Japanese Government voluntarily abolished the "picture brides" system (Japanese women who became wives by proxy) even though the "gentlemen's agreement" entitled them to come.

In June 1923 the Japanese-American Relations Committee of Tokyo, realizing that the anti-Japanese movement might endanger international relations, suggested that a joint high commission be established to study the question of Japanese immigration to the United States. The leaders of the anti-Japanese crusade in California objected and as a substitute they agreed to coöperate in an American survey which was being conducted under the leadership of Professor R. E. Park of the University of

Chicago for the Institute of Social and Religous Research of New York City, which though contributing to broader understanding actually affected no solution of the immediate problem.

Even as late as February 1924 Japan expressed her readiness to do all in her power to meet America's will in every possible way. Foreign Minister K. Matsui stated officially that Japan was "particularly anxious for American good-will" and that she was "ready to discuss the matter of restriction or exclusion anew, which should be arranged by mutual consideration and consent in agreement, as is customary, instead of through a needlessly arbitrary *ex parte* action." (*New York Times*, Feb. 8, 1924, p. 5.)

In fact, all available official and unofficial information seems to confirm the judgment of E. Alexander Powell that Japan was and is "genuinely, almost pathetically, anxious for American confidence and good will, and, in order to obtain them, she is prepared to make almost every concession that her self-respect will permit and that a fair-minded American can demand." (*Atlantic Monthly*, November 1921.)

VII

The anti-Japanese movement however had gained too great a momentum to be checked. The successes of the general restriction-of-immigration agitation since the World War added determination to

expression of "friendship and understanding" in the communication and evidently expecting salutary results, transmitted it on the following day to the Immigration Committees of both Houses. The Chairman of the Senate Committee, the late Senator Colt of Rhode Island, himself favorable to the Japanese, forwarded the letter to the Senate on the same day, obviously seeing nothing objectionable in it.

The Senate hall was practically empty when the Chief Clerk arose and perfunctorily read the letter. The concluding words were: "Relying upon the confidence you have been good enough to show me at all times, I have stated or rather repeated all this to you very candidly and in a most friendly spirit, for I realize, as I believe you do, the grave consequences which the enactment of the measure retaining that particular provision would inevitably bring upon the otherwise happy and mutually advantageous relations between our two countries."

VIII

Grave consequences! The clerk had scarcely read the last words when Junior Senator Shortridge, springing to his feet, said: It is an "extraordinary," a "specious, verbose communication. . . . I shall later make reply to the statements contained in this communication, which, in my judgment and according to my belief, based upon as accurate information as can be obtained, cannot be sustained."

Senior Senator Hiram Johnson also rose, inquiring whether the Secretary of State had made reply to this "astounding communication." But neither Senator appears to have perceived at this time the use to which the letter could be put. It was ordered printed and copies distributed to the Senate members.

"Grave consequences"—it was then clear! And that one phrase, evidently unwittingly used, brought into sharp fruition the efforts of twenty years or more. The Washington Conference with the good will it had fostered between the two nations, the recent earthquake which had scarcely stopped rocking Japan, the helpless condition of Japan in view of her economic relations "amounting to little short of dependence" upon the United States, these and every effort Japan had made to arrive at an amicable solution of the immigration problem were forgotten or consciously overlooked. In a perfectly civil communication Senators saw nothing but "veiled threats", a demand for "unqualified racial equality", nothing but an "international precedent."

On April 12 the day after the reading of the letter in the Senate, in the heat of the moment, the House passed the immigration bill, including the Japanese exclusion clauses, by a vote of 323 to 71, 37 not voting. On April 14 occurred the scene alluded to in the opening paragraphs of this chapter. On *Good Friday*, April 18, the bill passed the Senate with a vote of 62 to 6, 28 not voting.

While the act was in conference between the two Houses President Coolidge made an effort to postpone the application of the exclusion of Japanese clause to March 1, 1925, in order that the President might "negotiate with the Japanese Government in relation to the abrogation of the present arrangement on the subject." But leaders of the anti-Japanese movement bitterly opposed the suggestion. "It would surrender a sovereign right and give to foreign countries a power which the country has never conceded" declared the Majority Report of the House Committee. An immigration treaty "is contrary to our form of government" said the late Mr. Raker of California before the House, ". . . it is yielding of sovereign power . . .; it is getting down on the knees and getting the President to enter into a treaty that we may waive our rights, that we may fail to do our duty, that we may violate the Constitution; that we might become subservient to a foreign country. . . ."

In the Senate, Senators Lodge, Robinson, Shortridge and others opposed the proposal of the President. Senator Reed of Pennsylvania upheld the President on the ground that exclusion of Japanese as provided for in the bill would make the task of Christian missionaries in Japan harder and our foreign relations more difficult. The temper of Congress was not unlike that which led it to act on the Literacy Test. Then in the face of four Presidential vetos Congress seemed to cry "The Literacy Test right or wrong." Now it was in a like mood. It would not brook interference from the people, the press, the Japanese Ambassador, the State Department, the opponents in both Houses, the President. The Japanese *must* be excluded, excluded only in this manner and excluded they were.

But still there was hope. "There is another [Easter] hope stirring the minds of many," wrote the *New York Times* on Easter Day. "It is that the President will veto the bill which embodies this hasty and ill-tempered affront to a friendly people." This Easter hope, however, was not fulfilled. The President did affix his signature, although he expressed his disapproval of the exclusion clause; and President Coolidge goes down into history as the President who officially approved an act embodying such a far reaching expression of race discrimination.

IX

Those who upheld this act of Congress did so on three principal grounds. First, they maintained that the law brought our immigration legislation into harmony with our naturalization laws. The Japanese, however, were already excluded from United States citizenship and they would still have been excluded if, under the quota, 146 of them had been permitted to enter each year.

Second, the act of Congress was justified on the

ground that if Japan had been permitted to confer about the matter of Japanese exclusion that presently there would have come other nations: China, India, Afghanistan, Baluchistan and many other small states demanding the same privilege. It needs to be noted, however, that these people had already been excluded for several years, while Japan had been under the "gentlemen's agreement" and yet none of them had asked that they too be placed under a "gentlemen's agreement."

The third contention was that a continuance of Japanese immigration might have resulted in another race problem in this country, like that of the Negro in the south. This argument has more validity than the others. But it needs to be observed that the Negroes were brought in in *large numbers* when the population of this country was exceedingly small, whereas the quotas would have allowed only 146 to enter each year when the population was 110,000,000 or more. Moreover, it must be recalled that what was asked for was not that even 146 Japanese a year be admitted, but rather that the United States and Japan be given an opportunity to confer in order that exclusion, if it were to be brought about, be effected in a spirit of friendship and mutual understanding. Furthermore, even if Congress had allowed 146 Japanese to enter each year under the quotas still the comparison with the negro problem does not seem valid. The Japanese

are among the most advanced people of the world
to-day, and difficult as is the problem of their presence in the West, there seems to be no justification
for the contention that the Japanese would have
created a problem similar in kind or magnitude to
that created by the coming of the Negroes in the
seventeenth century. "Too bad", remarked Senator
King of Utah, "if we—110,000,000—are unable to
withstand an untoward aggression or influence on
the part of 146 Japanese."

It is a mark of the respect which the people of
the United States entertain for the Japanese that
the overwhelming majority of Americans definitely
disapproved the manner in which Congress excluded
the Japanese.

Ambassador Woods in the letter already cited
pronounced "the Japanese exclusion act an international disaster of the first magnitude. . . . And
the tragedy lies in the fact that Congress could have
secured what it felt needful, and yet have secured
it in a way that would have avoided affronting
Japan."

The *New York Times* commenting editorially on
Easter Morning 1924 said: "The action of the
United States Senate last Friday is one that has
marked it this year as a day of shame and made
another Black Friday. . . . The manner in which

on this very day we have dealt with a friendly people in the East, whose commercial intercourse with the rest of the world we compelled, will discredit the name by which we are collectively known. It is not that immigration has been restricted. This could have been accomplished in a friendly way. We could do unto them as we should wish them to do unto us."

The Christian Science Monitor (May 21, 1924) said: "It is certain that the method is highly offensive to a Nation with whom the United States should take especial pains to remain on terms of peace. . . . It was therefore as unwise as it was discourteous for the United States Congress to brand this intelligent and progressive Japanese people with a stigma only applicable to the most uncivilized and barbarous Asiatic tribes."

Mr. Milton W. Sutton, speaking under the auspices of the National Security League from radio station WHN in New York said: "When this proposal [that the Japanese should be treated on the same basis as the people of other races] was pressed at one of the sessions of the Senate Committee, the unanswerable reply was that the application of the quota to the Japanese would recognize them as the racial equal of European groups and of ourselves, and that this would be intolerable. . . . If we have such a desperate time granting freedom and equality of opportunity to the Japanese who are at this particular junction the most educated, progressive and

Americanlike of all the people of the East, what is to become of us when the millions of China, India and Africa, to-morrow and the day after, struggle to their knees and then to their feet and finally stand facing us eye to eye, claiming a place with us as our peers? . . . If we cannot make this adjustment, there is nothing ahead but disaster. It is not Japan, but *America* that is on trial in this present situation."

We might go on quite indefinitely citing the expressions of disapproval the action of Congress evoked. Leading newspapers in nearly all parts of the country pronounced themselves against it. The *New York Herald Tribune* declared the act "an unnecessary affront to Japan"; the *Washington Post* said: "There was no occasion for the disagreeable happening, no difference in principle requiring it, and no exigency excusing it." The *News Bulletin* of the Foreign Policy Association stated that "persistent agitation, inadvertently abetted by diplomatic ineptitude and culminating in Senatorial hysteria, threatens needlessly to wreck the most important achievement of the Washington Conference." A survey showed that forty out of forty-four newspapers published east of Chicago criticized the act of Congress.

A group of 30 Chancellors, Presidents and Former Presidents of leading American universities and colleges, including Charles W. Eliot, David Starr Jordan, W. W. Campbell, cabled Japan expressing regret over "the inconsiderate action of the American Congress, which does not represent the sentiments of the American people toward Japan." A group of prominent New York citizens, including Henry W. Taft, George W. Wickersham, Thomas W. Lamont, Darwin P. Kingsley and J. B. Millett sent a similar cable to the American-Japanese Society in Tokio.

X

It is perhaps difficult to realize how deep a wound the exclusion clause inflicted upon the soul of Japan and the entire East; it is always difficult for those inflicting an injury to realize its effects. On July 1, 1924, designated as "Humiliation Day", popular meetings of protest were held in many cities throughout Japan; in Tokio alone there were twelve such meetings, the largest beginning at 2 P.M. and lasting without a break until 10 P.M., the audience ranging from 5,000 to 12,000. In the weeks immediately following occurred the self-immolation of a Japanese, the demonstration made by some 10,000 Japanese former service men at the national military shrine, the boycotting of American goods, particularly films, the protests of Japanese Christians and their demand for severance of connection with American churches and the disturbances caused by the "rorin". Official Japan, however, has maintained a spirit of utmost dignity although of firmness.

The Japanese Diet met in special session on July 1, 1924, the day the law went into effect, and adopted strong but dignified expressions of protest. In January, 1925, Japan's Foreign Minister, Baron Shidehara, while reviewing Japan's international relations before the Japanese Diet, said: "Until our just contentions have been given satisfaction, we shall maintain our protests and shall use our best endeavors to seek an amicable adjustment of the question and to ensure forever the traditional friendship between the two nations." In January 1926, the same official said: "I only desire to make it clear that we remain unchanged in our feelings of deep regret at this particular clause [exclusion clause], which seems to us to be irreconcilable with the rules of international comity and justice."

On the return of "Humiliation Day," July 1, 1926, an editorial in the *Mainichi,* a daily morning paper published in Osaka, having a circulation of 1,250,000, declared: "We assert that the pain is becoming more and more acute. . . . Japan and her people will never forgive nor forget the insult and injustice to which they have been subjected. . . . The mental wounds which we sustained cannot be healed. The immigration question is not a problem of statistics. The honor and prestige of this Empire are involved . . . International democracy . . . will not permit her to be humiliated by disgraceful discrimination . . . It is our firm conviction that justice will be victorious finally. We are confident that Americans will be aroused to international justice and will correct their mistakes."

Americans who know Japan at first hand understand how deeply the matter goes. William Axling, a leading missionary and author of note, who was in Japan at the time the exclusion law was passed, wrote: "Japan's reaction to America's exclusion move is not so much resentment as it is the dire disappointment and poignant grief that a friend feels when a friend has failed to play fair. And Japan is not thinking of herself alone. She is looking out and considering the whole future of the Pacific. Japan is wondering whether brotherhood is going to be broadcast across this world of ours, or whether race shall stand against race and color against color."

Yonejiro Ito, a graduate of the University of Michigan and President of the largest shipping company in the Far East, in an interview he gave George Marvin, an American correspondent, said: "The cause for mutual prejudice and dislike between white and yellow races lies in the lack of understanding, more perhaps in the lack of opportunities to make ourselves understood by one another. American exclusion is a matter of racial prejudice . . . due to unreasonable apprehension arising from a complete misunderstanding which blinds the eyes of Americans to the true national spirit of Japan to-day."

The removal of this misunderstanding constitutes one of the principal tasks before the present and the coming generation. And this can only be done by frankly keeping before us the facts; and that is the reason why this story has been told in detail. The will seems to exist among the people of both countries to remove the misunderstanding. "Whether the knot that has been so bunglingly tied," remarked the *Chronicle* of New York at the time, "can be untied and good feeling restored all round, or whether the knot must be cut in order to get rid of it, depends upon the willingness of each of the parties to the controversy to meet the others at least halfway." That Japan has been and still is willing to go halfway few Americans would question. Will America meet Japan halfway?

Japan has at no time asked, nor does she now ask, for unrestricted immigration to this country, but only for a just and considerate treatment. The Japanese people recognize the wisdom and expediency of excluding Asiatic laborers, on the grounds of possible economic competition and race conflict. They only ask that they be relieved from discourtesy and humiliation, since their people cannot and will not accept the stigma of inferiority merely on account of race.

We need also to bear in mind and respect the demand of the Pacific Coast and indeed of all

America that protection be afforded against the dangers of a possible large Asiatic immigration.

The plan presented to Congress by former Secretary Hughes seems to be the most feasible: namely, to put Japan, at least, under the quota. Should this be done, the number of Japanese who would be admitted as immigrants annually, under the National Origins provision of the immigration law, which goes into effect July 1, 1928, would be one-tenth of one per cent of 150,000, or 150. Were China and India to be placed under the quota, they would secure only the minimum of one hundred each. These figures would include also all immigration to the United States of members of the white race born in those countries.

This change, while meeting the American requirements, would at the same time remove the much resented element of race discrimination; would help all intelligent and informed Asiatics to feel that after all the American people *do* practise the fundamental principles of justice and fair play, of humanity and brotherliness. And such a belief entertained by a half of mankind would surely have powerful influence in maintaining amicable relations between the people of the Pacific and in preserving a permanent peace the world over.

CHAPTER IX

RESTRICTION'S FEARS AND HOPES

We in the United States have a freer and fuller
opportunity than any other nation to choose our
course. . . . Our country is young. It is rich. It
may grow to twice its present numbers before the
economic pressure becomes disastrous. These days
of grace are valuable, immeasurably valuable. And
I have a buoyant hope . . . that before the zero hour
strikes the leaven of education will have so permeated
the masses as to lead them to accept without question
the wisdom of keeping the population standardized
at a figure far below the level which submerges joy
and comfort. If they do, they will be able to feel
the pride of having put up an *intelligent* struggle,
and far in the dim distance their descendants can
depart smiling when they must.

—*Edward Murray East.*

I

THE restriction of immigration movement may be
likened to a great drama and the events of 1924 nar-
rated in the foregoing pages to a climax. In this
drama both *fears* and *hopes* dominated the American
actors. Fears! The ever widening stream of immigrants, their concentration in the industrial sections
of the country, the rise of sizable Little Italies, Little
Russias and Polands, of Ghettos and Chinatowns all
over the nation, the development of pools of "alien"

influence in politics and religion, the competition of
foreigners in the labor market, the alleged degen-
eracy, criminality, dependency and deficiency of the
"new" immigrant, the rumors of the growing influence of "alien radicals" in labor movements, the
alleged crimes of the "aliens" against the government and the capitalistic order and "the throngs
literally standing on the shores of the Old World
looking toward America"—these, dramatized, made
vivid and kept before the public by constant repeti-
tion during several decades created fears, or "pictures in the head" as Walter Lippmann would call
them.

That there were large germs of truth at the root
of these fears no one can deny. The presence of large
numbers of newly arrived immigrants with their comparatively low standards of living did actually offer
a competition to the laborer already in this country,
did place the latter at disadvantage, retard labor
organization, delay improvement in conditions of
labor and hold back the advance in the standards of
living. Again it is obvious that the influx of immigrants did stimulate the development of antisocial
political influences, while the growth of the slums
created serious social problems.

These germs of truth, however, appear to have
been greatly exaggerated. The committee established by Congress in 1924 to compute the national
origins reports that of the total white population of

94,820,915 in 1920, 53,532,345 were of immigrant stock and 41,288,570 of original native stock. According to the 1920 Census nearly fourteen million persons of foreign birth were residing in this country or approximately the same percentage in our total population as for several decades. Moreover, immigrants are still coming, are still making more or less equivalent net deposits in our population and yet the United States are here leading a somewhat normal life, apparently untouched by any pernicious [sic] "alien" influences.

These immigration fears, however, have without much doubt been responsible for certain remarkable changes in the attitudes of the American people.

Thus, for instance, H. G. Wells found in 1906 that a generosity and a nobility of sentiment made of "every American above forty, and most of those below that limit . . . an enthusiastic advocate of unrestricted immigration." In 1927 it is difficult to find a high school pupil who does not entertain an antagonistic attitude toward immigration and the immigrant.

Again, not many years ago, notes Professor Fetter of Princeton University, Americans had a natural sympathy for the oppressed of other lands; and it was their pride that they could extend a helping hand to the needy and the oppressed of other lands. The "wish to share with others the blessings of freedom and economic plenty . . . [was] a part of our

national heritage . . . the product of many generations of American experience." *Then* the American
accepted with considerable satisfaction the fact that
he was the product of the fusion of many "races".
To-day he regards with disfavor the idea that
America is the land of refuge; he definitely repudi-
ates the melting-pot concept; he conducts prolonged
investigations, as in the case of the Laughlin report,
for the sole purpose of *proving* that what the melting-
pot contains is mostly dross and the procedure which
led to it a grave mistake. He considers all racial
mixtures blunders and all migrating peoples a
menace.

Moreover, the core of the very promise of
America, namely, that a man shall be estimated or
valued not by what his forefathers were and did, but
by his own present worth—even this is threatened.
One of the great achievements of the American
Fathers was that they deliberately destroyed the old
caste system which made of society a sort of three
story establishment. Of the three great words then
ringing throughout the world, Liberty, Equality and
Fraternity, "America selected Equality as her key-
stone." To-day, on the other hand, there are many
who would destroy this essentially American idea.
They claim that only persons of certain *antecedents*,
of specific "races" or countries are worthy of membership in the national family. These alone would
find favor, all others are "scum of the earth". Many

of the *leaders* of public thought, those who are shaping the future of America, teachers, students, writers, professional men repudiate the ideal of equality. They declare it false in premise, contrary to the realities of life, worthless and base. They now emphatically declare that the American Fathers were wrong; men are not created equal nor can they expect to have an equal opportunity in the struggles of life.

It is, of course, quite possible that this is only a passing phase of public thought. For among the more enlightened one still encounters those who remain unmoved by "scares". Especially among the humbler classes, in the smaller communities and country districts one often meets Americans, native born Americans of American extraction, who breathe tolerance and good will, who still cling to the old-fashioned idea that "a man is a man, for a' that and a' that"; Americans who still believe that a person should be judged by individual and personal worth and not categorically condemned because he happens to be of a certain "race", color, creed or political belief. And it is quite possible that as the years pass we shall largely regain the ground we have lost; and as the strain and stress of war relax their strangle hold upon us we shall swing back to a more normal and constructive attitude and arrive at the conclusion that the American Fathers were not *all* wrong and we *all* right.

II

Turning now to the promises of the restriction movement, we find them to be mainly two: a restricted immigration will bring the United States (1) a greater economic well-being and (2) a stronger racio-cultural unity than it now enjoys.

Herbert Croly in *The Promise of American Life* expresses the first of these perhaps better than any one else. "The native American, like the alien immigrant, conceives the better future which awaits himself and other men in America as fundamentally a future in which economic prosperity will be still more abundant and still more accessible than it has yet been here or abroad. No alteration or attenuation of this demand has been permitted. . . . The promise, which bulks so large in their patriotic outlook, is a promise of comfort and prosperity for an ever-increasing majority of good Americans."

This "promise of comfort and prosperity" can be attained only or chiefly by a comparative sparsity of population, or, in other words, by a favorable man-to-land ratio. With a sparsity of population the people will be able to enjoy more of the open spaces. They will make greater use of machinery. This in turn will result in a greater productivity per unit of population, in more natural resources and food supply per capita, higher wages, a shorter work day, more leisure, higher standards of living and a more satisfying life for the masses. In short, a comparative sparsity of population promises all those elements which go to make up an enviable national situation.

The second large hope of the restriction movement is that by permitting primarily immigrants of northern and western Europe to enter, the United States will be enabled to retain or regain a unity of "race" and culture.

This country, say those entertaining this view, was founded chiefly by Anglo-Saxons and has been able to attain the large degree of unity and culture it now enjoys primarily because those elements predominated. The presence of large numbers of alien "races" or peoples threatens that unity and culture. Therefore if we allow only northwestern Europeans to enter we will keep a oneness of purpose and development and this in turn will preserve for the United States prosperity and well-being.

The Eugenics Committee of the United States put it as follows: "On the whole, immigrants from northwestern Europe furnish us with the best material for American citizenship and for the future up-building of the American race. They have higher living standards than the bulk of the immigrants from other lands; average higher in intelligence, are better educated, more skilled, and are, on the whole, better able to understand, appreciate and support our form of government. . . .

"It is not here a question of racial superiority of northwestern Europeans or of racial inferiority of southeastern Europeans. It is simply a question as to which of these two groups of aliens, as a whole, is best fitted by tradition, political background, customs, social organization, education and habits of thought, to adjust itself to American institutions and to American economic and social conditions; to become, in short, an adaptable, homogeneous and helpful element in our American national life."

III

These, then, briefly stated are the two larger promises of restriction. And they do make a great appeal. Close analysis, however, makes us wonder whether we are not expecting too much of the restriction movement, whether we are not making a fetish of it or expect it to be a panacea for all our ills. The first promise, for example, is based upon a purely materialistic concept of national well-being. It says in substance that a nation's good life is mainly a matter of economic prosperity and that economic prosperity is chiefly a matter of possession of large amounts of land and natural resources in proportion to population.

Few students of the modern world would question that economic well-being does confer benefits upon the life of nations. On the other hand few indeed are the scholars who do not see the inherent dangers of a purely materialistic civilization. Great thinkers like Petrie tell us that in proportion as a nation comes into possession of great wealth and the power and sense of power which go with wealth that the people begin to weaken and that may lead to their undoing.[1]

There are others who tell us that we need not even turn to the past for instruction. If the signs of our own times are at all correctly read it would seem as if great wealth were gnawing at the very roots of the good life, throwing the nation into a state of mere motion, robbing us of a well rounded and poised living, giving nation and people a ruinous sense of security, an exaggerated idea of what economic power can do and setting us on the dangerous seas of imperialism.

It would lead too far afield for us to attempt to test the validity of these contentions. But if they are even relatively true it would seem as if the basic aim of restriction holds a promise which is a wolf in sheep's clothing. This does not mean that for that reason we should advocate the open door. Not at all! It simply means that restriction's promises are at least open to serious questioning.

Another contention is open to doubt: that restriction is necessary if economic prosperity is to be maintained or attained. We have already seen that the economic supremacy of the United States was attained during the very period when large numbers

[1] See the quotation at the close of this chapter.

of immigrants were coming into the country. As thoroughly an objective thinker as Professor Levasseur wrote in 1884: "It is owing exclusively to its enormous alien population that the United States is at the present day in a position to take rank with the great European powers." This statement may contain an exaggeration and yet even the most conservative statement could not possibly fail to grant that immigrants have contributed greatly to the industrial development of this country; contributed not alone by their numbers but also by their age, sex and training. The vast majority of them have been males, "strong healthy adults who became a direct (and immediate) addition to the producing and wealth increasing elements of the country." (See *American Economic Review*, March 1927.)

The difficulty is still with us even if we maintain with General Francis A. Walker that this is not so; that immigrants have not materially contributed to the economic well-being of the United States, and that the United States would still have produced approximately the same population and wealth, if not one immigrant had arrived after the founding of the nation. Of course it would be exceedingly difficult to prove this point either one way or the other. (However, see *Social Forces*, September 1926.) But if we accept General Walker's opinion as valid we are then forced into the position that restriction offers only an apparent solution of our problem. For if immigration in the long run does not affect the rate of population growth one way or the other, how will *restriction* produce a favorable land-to-man ratio? If population will increase at approximately the same rate regardless of immigrants will not the results be that the land-to-man ratio will be virtually the same, immigration or no immigration?

Moreover we often fail to recognize that a true ratio between man and land does not consist in mere density, but rather in the degree to which the land is distributed among the people, the extent to which it is utilized and the degree to which natural resources are turned into consumption goods. Mere possession of land is of doubtful value. A vast tract of uncultivated land may keep one man poor, while a comparatively small amount of land and natural resources intensively cultivated and utilized may make another man well-to-do.

Nor can we maintain that the standard of living is primarily a matter of physical comforts, without running into dangers. Comforts do, of course, produce a certain degree of the good life. But it is a serious question whether in America we are not greatly exaggerating their capacity to produce true individual or national well-being. Los Angeles without doubt has many more automobiles and bath tubs in proportion to population than Paris; but it is at best questionable whether Los Angelenos enjoy more of the good life than do the Parisians.

Moreover a high standard of living is not necessarily a matter of low density of population, otherwise thinly settled countries and regions would invariably have high standards and thickly settled ones have a low standard. Back Valley would be a much more desirable place to live in than Boston, and Podunk than Washington. A true standard of living is a matter of efficient production, wholesome living, a chance to work and security in work, good working conditions, well apportioned income, rational use of income. More than mere possession of wealth, more than a favorable man-to-land ratio, true national well-being is the result of an equitable distribution of income, intelligent use of leisure, a moral and spiritual character and attitudes which enrich life. And it is very difficult to see how any of these can be connected with restrictions.

It cannot be too often stressed that this does not necessarily argue for an open door policy; it does point out, however, that the restriction movement has led us to place our faith in wooden horses and in kites that have no wings.

IV

When we turn to the more tangible economic improvements which restriction of immigration promises we are more nearly in a position to evaluate objectively. First it promises certain definite and immediate things to the working man:

With a comparatively small number of immigrant workers coming into this country we may expect to have a scarcity and inelasticity of labor. The large number of immigrant laborers who used to come to the United States in periods of expansion and return to Europe in slack times will no longer come. Instead, only a comparatively small number will be admitted as *permanent* members of our industrial organization. As a result a stability will develop in the labor market which in turn will enable Labor to demand and receive a larger share of the profits of and management in industry. This in time will result in shorter hours, higher wages and greater consumption power.

This will inevitably lead to high priced labor, although not necessarily high cost labor. The American worker, already highly efficient, will become even more so and in proportion as he is used in connection with a large volume of land and capital he will produce a larger per capita output, which in turn will make for lower prices and living cost for the population as a whole.

A restriction of immigration will also tend to produce a more even distribution of industrial enterprise over the various portions of the United States. In the past European immigrant laborers have in the main gone to the Atlantic seaboard. With their curtailment during the last few years the rise of wages has been most rapid in that section. This in turn will lead to the shifting of industry from the Atlantic seaboard to other portions of the country, a movement which has already occurred to an appreciable extent.   Benjamin M. Anderson, an industrial expert, writing on this very point states: "In cotton textiles, notably, there has been a very decided shifting from New England, where wages are very high, to the South, where wages are still much lower. Labor, moreover, has been shifting from the South to the North, and from the country to the industrial centers.   These movements will tend to go on, with the resultant leveling up of wages in the interior of the country, and ultimately a leveling down of wages on the Atlantic seaboard."   While of course high freight rates and a depression of agriculture have contributed, the slackening of the flow of European labor has no doubt been the principal factor in producing these results.

Whether these more or less immediate improvements will result from our immigration restriction policy depends upon a number of factors.   It depends first of all upon whether or not Mexican labor comes to fill the gap left in the labor market by the absence of European labor.   We have already observed that Mexicans and other labor from the New World tend to increase as European immigrants decrease.   And since Mexicans, by the comparative permanency with which they remain in this country, offer an even sharper and more constant competition to American labor, it is not impossible that no great improvement will follow, except possibly in the East where the Mexican laborer is a negligible factor.

Again it is quite probable that American capital will flow into those European countries which have an abundance of low priced labor. American capital will without doubt and in any event move increasingly into Europe in proportion as economic conditions become stabilized on that continent. But this movement may be intensified by our immigration policy. If this proves to be the case the conditions of labor in this country will not be materially improved, since American labor will still be subjected to virtually the same competition, one point removed.

Furthermore, the hoped for improvements will depend upon the changes which will actually occur in relative wages, prices and production. If labor continues to leave agriculture at the same rate as at present in answer to the demand of manufacturing, agricultural output will in time necessarily decrease except as machinery is substituted. Even this will tend to produce relative higher prices for food products and higher living costs for the industrial laborers as well as for the public as a whole. Even in industry a general improvement will largely depend upon whether American capitalists are willing to use land and capital with comparative lavishness and labor with greater and greater reserve.

It is too early to measure the economic results of the restrictionist policy and yet it is interesting to note that some quite significant facts are already available and were presented at the annual meeting of the American Economic Association in December 1926. (*American Economic Review*, March 1927.) The principal economic effects of restriction are: the increased negro migration to northern industrial districts; the greatly increased Mexican migration to the United States; the acceleration of the movement from rural districts to urban centers and the improvement in industrial methods and equipment and efficiency.

A notable increase has occurred "in total production and in production per man hour and in real wages." The ratio between the wages of skilled and unskilled labor, however, remains practically the same as at the close of the war. The mechanization of industry is not attributed to restriction of immigration, while the machine building industry seems to have been influenced by the reduced labor supply. One now finds "the self-feeding wagon-loader, the snow-loader, the narrow trench digger, for pipe lines, conduits, etc., where Italian labor had formerly been used. The contractor is more confident he can get his job done if he is using a machine than human labor." Organized labor maintains that restriction has prevented a large amount of unemployment, led employees to eliminate "the brute-like work of human beings", and resulted in an increase in insurance, motor cars, et cetera.

The increase in Mexican immigration has led to the most far reaching result. This element contributed less than 50,000 (0.6 per cent of the total) in the decade 1901-10; 219,000 (3.8 per cent of the total) in the decade 1911-20 and 279,000 (9.5 per cent of the total) in the past six years. This increase in Mexican immigration, most of which consisted of unskilled laborers, has produced revolutionary results in agriculture, particularly in Texas. The present low price of cotton, the development of large landed estates (latifundia) and the bringing of large new tracts under cultivation are all attributed more or less directly to the presence of large numbers of Mexicans in the Southwest.

It is also too early to determine how far the restriction policy will affect the flow of American capital abroad. And yet changes have taken place which may possibly be related. The United States Bureau of Foreign and Domestic Commerce reports that the total value of foreign corporate securities bought in the United States in 1925 was nearly four times as great as in 1924. European issues alone in 1925 were fourteen times as great as in 1924. (*The Balance of International Payments in* 1925.) This same Bureau informs this writer under date of May

24, 1927 that there has been a general increase in
the net amount of American capital leaving this
country since 1924, as shown by the following table:

Period	Nominal Capital	Refunding	Nominal Value (net)	No. of Issues
1924:				
First half...	$379,700,000	$153,800,000	$225,900,000	
Second half.	830,100,000	178,000,000	652,100,000	
Total	$1,209,800,000	$331,800,000	$878,000,000	108
1925:				
First half...	$551,591,000	$114,325,000	$437,266,000	
Second half.	723,376,000	129,435,000	593,941,000	
Total	$1,274,967,000	$243,760,000	$1,031,207,000	152
1926:				
First half...	$596,163,150	$83,695,300	$512,467,850	
Second half.	722,391,700	100,199,900	622,191,800	
Total	$1,318,554,850	$183,895,200	$1,134,659,650	214
1927:				
First quarter	$377,472,700	$16,757,700	$360,715,000	73

When compared with the decrease in European
immigration these figures suggest that a possible
correlation may exist between immigration and the
flow of capital.

V

On the "racial" side the restriction movement gives
us the promise that "race" purity will be realized as
soon as northwestern Europeans alone are admitted.
This promise, of course, rests upon the large assump-

tion that "races" and peoples possess widely divergent capacities and that their mixture is highly undesirable. It also rests upon the contention that "new" immigrants are somewhat inferior people. It would indeed lead us too far afield to attempt to test these underlying assumptions; we may say, however, that in so far as we have any data they seem to point in the opposite direction.

Anthropological measurements indicate that the differences between the extremes within any one race is greater than between the means of any two races. Again, Professor Franz Boas of Columbia University has shown that mixture of types has occurred in the past without detrimental effects. He cites the mixture of Iberian, Celtic, Teutonic and Moorish populations in the Spanish peninsula, the colonization of the Italian peninsula by Greeks, Celtic and Teutonic tribes, the intermixtures of racial stocks in the British Isles and similar mixtures, even greater, in Central Europe. "The actual conditions in the United States are, in many respects, analogous . . . the only difference being that the numbers involved are very much larger and that the whole process is more rapid because the social barriers which separate the migrating people from the natives are not as [sic] strong and enduring as they used to be." (*Current History*, Feb. 1927.)

The findings of Dr. Ales Hrdlicka, Curator of the Division of Physical Anthropology, United States

National Museum, would seem to indicate that the new immigrant shows no trace of inferiority. His studies of immigrants, made with the coöperation of the Public Health Service and covering twelve immigrant groups, "give no evidence that the mass of immigrants are bringing inferiority of the body, nor judging from the size of the head, inherent inferiority of the brain. . . . It may be soberly said, therefore, that, while certain areas of this country may become more or less colored by European strains, there is little danger that the American type will be altered for the worse, either physically or mentally, as the result of immigration, so long as we keep out the mentally abnormal and those in other ways undesirable."

Even if we assume, however, that new immigrants *do* differ materially from those who came before, we are still confronted with the fact that we have no proof that homogeneity (assuming that it could be brought about), would produce superior types. The reply usually given to this statement is: since we have no evidence "about the value of race mixture, the wise policy is to avoid it. . . . The line of safety is indicated by the good old maxim—'in case of doubt, don't.' "

But that is precisely it: "In case of doubt, don't." Such proofs as we have favor race mixtures. Historically race mixture has been at the very root of the development of the human race. Men of every tribe, nation and race, upon moving from territory to territory, have continually intermixed. In fact migrations with their concomitant intermixture of peoples are inextricably interwoven with the formation of states, the survival of institutions, the mobility of labor, the utilization of productive forces, and every large advance in civilization. (Encyclopaedia Brittanica, *Migration*) England itself is largely the product of intermixture; the fusion of new racial strains admittedly played a large part in making that country one of the leading nations of the modern world. And the United States themselves, whatever may be their future policy, surely have been in no small measure the product of intermixture. The *doubt*, then, seems to be against those who, through legislation enacted in the heat of postwar times, would *compel* a people to depart from the practice of centuries. Not that we should fear conscious departure from what has been. But it seems quite clear that the restrictionist policy can offer no proof for its fundamental contention relative to the desirability of race purity.

On the cultural side the restrictionist promises definite social and political advance. "The spirit of American nationality" writes the editor of the *Chicago Tribune*, "is going to have a new birth, is going to be harmonized and intensified as it has not been perhaps for half a century. . . . The new policy assures the American future to the American people.

We shall never be without the inspiration of other people and other cultures. But we shall not have them undermining our American structure or imposing upon us as self-conscious alien forces demoralizing the harmonious evolution of our national character."

The question here arises: Do we have evidence that cultural pluralism and harmonization produces inferior results? Or would it be more true to say that a self-generated, self-determined and self-centered culture is much more liable to lead to disaster? Recent events of world-wide magnitude are too vivid in our memories to need specific mention of what may overtake nations which follow the god of intensified nationality. If the history of civilization has been at all correctly written it would seem to point to the conclusion that a self-centered culture is capable of driving a people headlong toward the precipices of destruction and of setting a whole civilization into flames.

If a restrictionist policy should contribute in the smallest way to the creation of self-centered, haughty and belligerent attitudes, it is not impossible that it will become one of the most indomitable enemies of a nation that has held a place of honor and pre-eminence in the family of nations.

The restrictionist also promises that *tolerance* will ensue as a result of the policy he advocates. There are racial groups, he contends, "whose coming greatly complicates the situation for those of their race already here"; if the former are kept out good will and understanding will gradually displace intolerance. But, as Glenn Frank points out, it is difficult to see how a movement which finds its very inspiration in assuming and proclaiming its superiority over large segments of the world's population, can possibly yield tolerance. There are already in this country some fourteen millions of foreign born persons and forty-five millions or more of foreign or mixed parentage and who in one degree or another are related to the very "races" stigmatized as inferior. "Whether we regard it as subtle poison or the elixir of life, foreign blood is in the veins of our national life. We face a problem of social procedure as well as a problem of biology and anthropology." Will the policy of discriminating against certain races and peoples "tear apart the racial strands of our national life?" Will it "make outcasts of all but our Nordic folk?" Will it lead to "an ugly century of race hatred, social bigotry, and organized intolerance, with the spirit of the Nordics poisoned in the process?" (*Century Magazine*, May 1924.)

Finally, it is also claimed that the barring of "alien" peoples will in time produce conditions in this country which will become an inspiration to the other nations of the world. Our prosperity will become a beacon light to all the world and the rest of man will go and do likewise. The fallacy of this contention is too obvious to need discussion. The argument is like that which a very wealthy man might advance. Having come early upon the scene and having acquired vast domain and inclosed them within a wall, he now says to the poor man on the outside: "Behold what I have done! Go and do thou likewise."

These are the promises the restrictionist policy gives us: it will bring unbounded prosperity for America of to-day and to-morrow; will lift the masses from sordidness and misery; will yield "racial" purity; will eliminate strife and bigotry; will create a world where peace and contentment abide.

But, says the English scholar, W. M. Flinders Petrie, and it makes us ponder: "So soon as each subject loses its archaism and reaches full freedom of expression, there is no more strife with difficulties and uncertainties of mode; then strife being ended, decay sets in shortly after. . . . Further, the accumulation of the facilities of life, or capital in every form, diminishes the need for striving. There is much less worth striving for, there is so much more to enjoy without strife. Hence, the easier life is rendered, the more easy is decay and degradation. The maximum of wealth must inevitably lead to downfall." (*Revolutions of Civilisation.*)

CHAPTER X

We are beginning to apply science to life. We have done with *laissez-faire*—which means, let things grow up. We are going to make them grow up. . . . There is not an element or feature of life that we cannot . . . raise to a vastly higher level. We are going to treat life as a scientific breeder treats plants. It shall all be plotted out, and its conditions scientifically studied, by a central brain. The idea of fighting it out and letting the better survive is the very opposite of science. Evolution guided by intelligence, constructive evolution, harmonious social coöperation—these are the ideals obviously thrust upon us by the very fact that intelligence now exists.—*Joseph McCabe.*

I

It might sound like baying at the moon to raise the question "What of the Future?" were it not for the fact that the immigration problem is far from settled. One has only to consult the Congressional Record for the 69th Congress, which closed on March 4, 1927, to discover how alive that question still remains. In the first session of that Congress no less than 106 bills dealing with immigration and naturalization were introduced in the House and 48 in the Senate; and in the second session 36 in the House and 12 in the Senate.

In fact immigration has perhaps never been so "much with us, soon and late, getting and spending" as it has since the enactment of the 1924 law. The increase of immigration from contiguous territory, the problem of surreptitious and excess quota entries, the administrative difficulties arising from the enforcement of the law, the demand for more labor notably by the ranchers of California, the insistence upon the enactment of rigid deportation laws, the important decisions made by various courts, the problem of determining the "national origins"— these and other questions have kept immigration before us as much as at any time since the American Fathers referred to it in the Declaration of Independence and the Constitution.

The discussion of this chapter, therefore, is in keeping with the situation as it obtains at present and may obtain for some time in the future. It aims to cast a look toward the future for it is quite clear also that the movement of population into and out of this country will still continue and will be determined "not so much by the aberrations of statesmen as by the economic and social forces which are outside the orbit of political control." It is interesting to note in this connection that Mr. W. W. Husband, former Commissioner General of Immigration and later Assistant Secretary of Labor, wrote an essay as late as 1925 entitled *A Rational Immigration Policy.* It is possible, then, that reason

may still prevail and a constructive immigration
policy may find its way into the statute books.

There is still another reason why we are justified
in raising the question "What of the Future?" and
that is found in the fact that the most desirable features of the present immigration law are the result
of years of efforts. In truth it is a matter of common knowledge that it takes scores of years before
legislators can see constructive light. So that it may
be possible that on some fair day we may make sufficient progress toward adopting a constructive
immigration policy.

The plea has been heard for many years for a
rational, constructive and comprehensive immigration policy, a policy which while safeguarding the
interests of the United States, would at the same
time attempt to preserve good will among nations.
Such a *constructive immigration policy* would consist of four major phases, *admission, distribution,
incorporation* and *international relations*. In the
present chapter we will consider the first of these,
admission, in Chapter XI distribution, Chapter XII
incorporation and the last chapter international
relations.

Before discussing *admission* it is necessary to call
attention to the large difference between a construc-

to explore the possibilities of the science of human measurement; that we are very far as yet from having devised methods for an accurate and scientific measurement of hereditary capacities or from having even reached a concensus of opinion as to what characteristics are desirable. But even in their present development we do have some means of determining with a degree of accuracy hereditary backgrounds and this means may be employed to advantage in determining whether a person should or should not be admitted.

On the side of mental capacity, it has been recognized for some time that intelligence tests should be substituted for the superficial and wholly inconclusive Literacy Test. The question which presents itself in this connection is that of determining how high in the scale of intelligence the exclusion-admission line should be drawn. It would seem reasonable that the dividing line should be set at a point which would insure the selection of immigrants of at least average intelligence. The army intelligence tests, it will be recalled, classified all those tested into seven groups, ranging from very inferior (E) through average (C) to very superior (A). Here again selection should be made so as to admit from A down rather than from E up and to keep as far as possible above the *median line.*

These tests also are far from perfect as means of determining native intelligence or present mental capacity, since there are personal equations and circumstances of time and place which intelligence tests have as yet not been able to measure. But these problems are receiving attention and as the tests are improved and internationalized, they will certainly prove of positive value. Even in their present state of development, however, the intelligence tests can be expected to produce results far superior to those obtained under the Literacy Test.

Another positive test which may possibly yield fruitful results is that which would deal with the social adaptability of an immigrant. The suggestion has been made that examination be made into "the reputation of the immigrant in relation to his home community." But here we run into dangers. Just what is meant by "reputation in relation to home community" is difficult to say; nor is there any way of determining with any degree of exactness when one's reputation is "good" and when "bad". It is a commonplace that many persons who have attained eminence in society were, in their early life, considered "bad" in their communities. Likewise a prospective immigrant might have the very worst of reputation in his home community for political or social reasons and yet possess qualities which under new conditions might produce the very best citizen. The

law now provides that the immigrant shall present
such evidence as is available to indicate whether or
not he has committed any crimes or whether in other
ways he has proven a social misfit. These should
be supplemented by positive tests which would show
the ability of the applicant to become a constructive
agent in the community to which he comes.

A test of economic fitness has also been advocated
although, curiously enough, not very widely. President Roosevelt favored it. In his message to Congress of December 3, 1901 he suggested that the
immigrant should measure up to certain standards
of economic fitness; he should be able to show
capacity to earn an American living and he should
have enough money to insure a decent start under
American conditions. "His standard of living," said
Roosevelt in *A Square Deal*, "should be such that he
will not, by pressure of competition, lower the standard of living of our own wage-workers; for it must
ever be a prime object of our legislation to keep
high the standard of living."

Canada employs such a standard of economic fitness. That country requires that the head of a
family shall bring with him $250 and for every
dependent member of his family an additional $125.
In its recent agreement with the Polish Government
Canada has specified the sums which different classes
of immigrants must possess in order to become candidates for admission. These provisions, aside from
serving as a test of economic ability, incidentally

perform another useful purpose: they encourage the coming of those who, having enough money ahead, will not be easily lured into already congested industrial centers or occupations, but who will tend to seek those sections of the country and those occupations for which they are best fitted, in which they are most needed and in which they will profit most.

III

The next important question is: shall these standards be applied categorically or as nearly as possible individually. On this point there is a wide divergence of opinion. Some uphold the principle of wholesale "racial" selection, as embodied in the present law; some would take the family as a unit, while others insist that the individual should be the unit of value. Legislation and popular opinion favor the first position, while those who view the matter objectively support the last.

Many leaders have taken a stand in favor of individual selection. The three Presidents who vetoed the Literacy Test, it will be recalled, clearly favored the selection of immigrants on an individual basis. Roosevelt also was of the belief that "we cannot afford to pay heed whether (the immigrant) is of one creed or another, of one nation or another. . . . What we should endeavor to find out is the individual quality of the individual man."

Professor Davie of Yale thinks that the "racial"

distinctions incorporated in the 1924 law "are necessarily arbitrary and are not conclusive." They
constitute "a clumsy method of effecting an end
which may be desirable. Our immigration policy as
applied to the white race should be put on an individual basis. We should admit the type of individual
who meets the standards we set, no matter whether
he comes from the north and west or the south and
east of Europe." (*A Constructive Immigration
Policy.*) And the Eugenics Committee of the
United States has gone on record as advocating a
"law establishing a sufficiently high educational,
moral and physical test to admit, say 10 per cent
of all applicants, quite independent of geography."

Such a method of *individual* selection, provided
the standards are high enough, are positive in aim
and operation and are applied impartially, would
unquestionably tend to select a higher type than
can be selected by the categorical classifications
incorporated in the 1924 law, which aims, as already
indicated, to eliminate only the lowest in the social
strata and then admit by geographical distribution.

A selection on the individual basis would have
the additional advantage of tending to eliminate
racial and national distinctions, which inevitably lead
to misunderstanding and friction. Under this system the six-foot tall Englishman would have no better or no less of a chance than the six-foot tall Slovak
and the five-foot-four Greek or Italian could not

claim that he was discriminated against if he were
not selected because of his deficient height.

IV

Of importance also is the question of numbers. Is
the policy incorporated in the law of 1924 satisfactory? This law, as we have seen, by percentage, fixes
the number at 164,667 until July 1, 1927, and there-
after at 150,000.[1] Does this method of fixing numbers commend itself as adequate or should some
other be devised by which immigration might even be
entirely suspended at times? Obviously, fixing numbers arbitrarily has nothing of the scientific or of the
logical in it. The needs of the country may and do
actually vary from time to time; accordingly a sound
immigration policy must take into consideration these
varying needs.

This principle of elasticity has been advocated by
some and vigorously opposed by others. Professor
Jeremiah W. Jenks, who has been a close student of
the immigration problem for many years, said before
the Senate Committee on Immigration in 1921: "The
conditions vary so from year to year and often even
from month to month, that any policy we should
adopt should be a flexible policy that can be adapted
to new conditions. . . . A law should lay down the general principles but should leave to administrative

[1] The application of this provision was, by act of Congress of
March 3, 1927, postponed for one year.

authority a considerable degree of discretion in the administration of the law itself." Various other individuals and representatives of organizations have made similar suggestions, as an examination of the records of the hearings before the Congressional Committees on Immigration show. W. W. Husband in the essay on *A Rational Immigration Policy* already mentioned, also advocates elasticity, with the proviso that the limit set by the law of 1921 should serve as a point of departure and less or more immigrants of this or the other type be admitted as the need of the time might dictate.

This raises the question as to method of administering this elastic provision. The suggestion has frequently been made that an Immigration Board, much in the nature of and having similar powers to those of the Interstate Commerce Commission or the Federal Reserve Board should be created. The function of this board might range from definitely regulative to merely advisory; but it would endeavor in any case to determine from time to time the actual needs of the country and to regulate within certain set limits the number and the classes to be admitted.

The first duty or function of such an administrative body would be of a fact-finding nature. It would, first of all, aim to secure the facts as to what kind of labor was needed, where, when, and to what extent. It would secure information almost continuously from the different parts of the country and

from the various industries; it would keep itself
informed on labor shortage and on unemployment.

This would not entail much if any new machinery.
A coördination of existing governmental agencies
would produce the result desired. If the Federal
Bureau of Labor Statistics extended its index of
employment to cover transportation, trade-mining
and quarrying, in addition to manufacturing as it
does at present, and if also it should coöperate with
the various State Bureaus of Labor it would in time
be able to construct national, state, regional and
occupational-group indices which would be of ines-
timable value in calculating the labor needs of the
United States at any particular time.

With such information at its disposal the Immigration Board would be able to determine with quite
a degree of precision just how many immigrants, if
any, should be admitted at a given time; it would be
able to direct those entering into those parts of the
country where they were most needed; it would
thereby do something toward preventing excessive
unemployment and prevent immigrants from taking
fruitless journeys. It is of value to note that Canada is operating under a system similar to the one
here suggested and is reaping excellent results.
Through the orders in Council the number of immigrants permitted to enter varies from time to time
and is coördinated with the occupational and numerical needs of that country.

V

Another important question remains: shall immigrants be examined at the ports of embarkation or at those of arrival? The former method of course recommends itself as the more logical, and the wonder is that it has not been adopted long before this. The law of 1924 looks in that general direction by its adoption of the visa system; and under it immigration "technical advisers" are operating in twenty American consulates abroad. But this, as already indicated, does not provide for a real examination of the prospective immigrant, but rather for a verification by American consular officials of certain documents presented by the immigrant. So that the real examination is still made at the ports of arrival.

The Secretary of Labor, the Commissioner General of Immigration, and numerous private individuals and organizations have repeatedly urged the examination of aliens abroad. Various experts consider the scheme practicable. Referring to the psychological tests, for example, Dr. Arthur Sweeny believes that such an examination "is feasible, inexpensive and simple. It is practical to examine groups of two or three hundred at one sitting, in less than an hour. All that is required is a staff of two or three trained psychologists at each port at which large numbers embark." For physical and other examinations other experts would be necessary, but in any event not a large staff, and for this reason United States officials deem the plan entirely workable. With a centralization of examination points this system would prevent the departure of many who cannot be admitted, remove the necessity of making examinations hurriedly, as frequently happens when large numbers of immigrants arrive at one port or at one time, and would, moreover, save the United States the expense of retaining immigrants for varying periods, as is done at present.

The objection is made that this would place too much power in a few persons too far away from the source of authority. A proper system of checks and balances exercised by the diplomatic head of the United States Government in each foreign country would insure that no more corruption would exist than may obtain at present.

Some European governments, however, have refused to permit United States officials to examine their subjects in their home territories. The United States Department of State some years ago communicated with a number of European governments and found that many of them were opposed to such a scheme. Italy in particular objected. The objection of these Governments no doubt were due, at least in part, to the chauvinistic attitude some American legislators have taken in regard to the immigration problem. However, objections are being removed and immigration "technical advisers" are already functioning in twenty consulates in the three Scandinavian countries, Great Britain, Germany, Poland and Belgium.   In time the governments of emigration countries without doubt will coöperate still further with the United States Government in making possible a real examination abroad.   In fact, Professor Jeremiah W. Jenks, drawing upon personal investigations made years back, stated before the Senate Committee that foreign governments would not only not object to the examination of prospective immigrants within the territories under their jurisdiction, but would on the contrary welcome our taking the initiative in the matter.   This question is closely related to the problem of international agreements and to this we shall return in the last chapter.   Our attention is now directed to the topic of distribution.

CHAPTER XI

> I should like the entrance into the United States to
> be a poem to all who come. . . . All the way across
> the sea I would make of every ship a school. . . . I
> should like to teach the strangers that there is a fair
> reward for hard struggle and an honest living wage
> for an honest day's work . . . I should like to point to
> the Goddess of Liberty and say that she welcomes all
> who come in her name, and she guarantees freedom
> to all who obey law. . . . I should like to tell them
> that they have nothing to fear in this country except
> their own frailties, that there are no barriers here but
> their own clannishness, and that the way to the best
> is open to all who walk reverently.
>
> —*Edward A. Steiner.*

I

THE wisdom of attempting to do something toward
distributing immigrants has been recognized for many
years. It was stressed as far back as the time of
the Industrial Commission (1898-1902), if not
earlier; and Commissioner General of Immigration F.
P. Sargent, one of the most constructively minded
encumbents of that office, spent several years calling
attention to it. In his annual report for 1903 he gave
it as his mature judgment that all that the immigration law then provided for could not compare in prac-

tical value with, nor could it "take the place of, measures to insure the distribution of the many thousands who come in ignorance of the industrial needs and opportunities of this country, and, by more potent law than that of supply and demand, . . . colonizing alien communities in our great cities."

Students of immigration, individual and associations of employers, state officials and public minded men of all kinds have repeatedly emphasized the need. In one of the most vigorous pronouncements made on the question the *Outlook*, in its issue of June 13, 1914, said editorially, "The absence of intelligent methods of distribution has led to the practical segregation of great numbers of newcomers into localities which are almost as definite in boundary as the old pales in medieval cities. With a lack of foresight which has been criminal in its stupidity we have brought in small armies of men and women ignorant of our language, laws, and habits, planted them in isolated colonies, done little or nothing to show them how to be Americans, left them to the leadership of agitators, and then, when they have become turbulent and lawless, we have accused them of violating the hospitality of the Nation. As a matter of fact, hospitality has never been offered them. They have been brought over in shiploads, carted like freight to distant points, and dumped in a mass like unsaleable human refuse. They have worked; they have not been Americanized."

II

The need is so obvious that the question naturally arises: why are not efforts being made to distribute immigrants? The principal reason is found in the opposition offered by restrictionists in general and organized labor in particular to any proposal of this nature. The first group has opposed any such move on the ground that a distribution of immigrants would inevitably lead to a stimulation of immigration and the latter because it would give rise to the danger of immigrants being taken from one part of the country to another in time of labor disturbances under the guise of "distribution".

Some efforts have been made, however, to distribute immigrants. Largely through the activity of Commissioner General Sargent, the Division of Information was organized in 1907, as part of the Bureau of Immigration, for the purpose of promoting "a beneficial distribution of aliens admitted to the United States." In compliance with the immigration law of 1907 under which it was instituted, the Division corresponded with state and town officials and local postmasters, gathered information regarding the resources, products and physical characteristics of each state and territory and established a system of post-card inquiry by which the needs for labor of the various communities could be ascertained periodically. Over two million cards were sent out, publicity was conducted through agricultural journals, and bulletins of information were published in several languages.

As a result a widespread interest was manifested. A number of states, notably Virginia, North Carolina, South Carolina, Tennessee, Alabama, Missouri, New York, Wisconsin and California, which had already conducted work along similar lines, showed a marked interest. In 1911 representatives of twenty-six states convened in Washington, D. C. on the invitation of the Division of Information to discuss ways and means for distributing immigrants. Ohio during the same year organized a Bureau of Farm Labor for the purpose of coöperating with the Federal Division. Progress was made also in other states.

At the time of the War, however, the Division of Information was reorganized and its effort directed toward supplying the wartime shortage of labor. When this country entered the War and the United States Employment Service was established, the Division of Information was merged with that Service, and at the close of the War both the Service and the Division of Information disappeared as effective agencies—thus bringing to naught the progress of years.

A number of private agencies have also given attention to the distribution of immigrants. Conferences of business men were held in the South from

1900 to 1905; three interstate conventions met in 1905 at Birmingham, Alabama, Nashville, Tennessee and Tampa, Florida and another at Jackson, Mississippi in 1910—all for the expressed purpose of devising ways and means for bringing desirable white immigrants to the South and otherwise effecting their distribution. The Federation for the Promotion of Sane and Liberal Immigration Laws was founded for the purpose of making Galveston a principal port of debarkation and the Mississippi Valley Immigration Company with a view of securing immigrant labor for public work throughout the South.

Philanthropic agencies likewise made definite efforts to distribute immigrants. Principal among these are the Immigrant's Free Labor Bureau, the Industrial Removal Office, the National Employment Exchange, the Joint Application Bureau, the Jewish Agricultural Society, Inc. (the Baron de Hirsch Fund), the National Liberal Immigration League and the Young Women's Christian Association.

All these efforts were successful in varying degrees. During the nine years of the independent existence of the Division of Information, 1907 to 1916, in round numbers 415,000 persons applied for positions, 200,000 for information alone. Of these 115,000 were actually placed, 29,000 of them as farm laborers. Of the total placed, 47,000 were aliens and 71,000 were either natives or naturalized citizens. The Division estimated that the information it gave out or the protection it furnished actually reached on an average five times as many persons as sought information during each year, by virtue of the fact that those who received information directly imparted it to others. The Poles and the Germans particularly appear to have availed themselves of the opportunities offered by the Division, with the Russians, Irish and Italians coming next.

Among the various private or philanthropic agencies The Jewish Agricultural Society, Inc. seems to have produced the most tangible results. Up to December 31, 1926, that Society had extended its activities to forty states, had made 8360 loans, totaling $5,310,215, and since 1918 had assisted 848 families, or approximately 4240 persons, to settle on the land.

When closely analyzed, however, all these efforts appear to have been somewhat unsuccessful, chiefly for the reason that they dealt with the problem in an artificial and sporadic manner. The Division of Information, for example, was unable to function properly because of the very terms of the law which created it. That law instructed the Division to distribute information among all *admitted* aliens who might *ask* for it at the immigration stations of the United States. In the very nature of the case this could not and did not produce the desired results. The Division soon discovered that the aliens would *not ask* for information. How could they ask for that which they had no knowledge even existed. Again, the Division was supposed to function primarily at the *immigration stations*. But giving out information at these points proved of no practical value, for the simple reason that immigrants, like all other travelers, are more or less excited at the time of arrival and are not in a mood to accept and peruse literature. Furthermore, such information as reached arriving aliens was too general: it described conditions of large districts or sections of the country, rather than impart specific, detailed information which might at the time or subsequently direct the immigrant to particular localities.

The lack of success on the part of the Division of Information contributed to the unsuccessful issue of state efforts, since in the absence of a strong coördinating agency, the activities of the states were more or less sporadic, artificial and uncorrelated. State efforts also failed because the various state agencies played up local interest rather than participated in a national wide movement. Here and there, however, the efforts of a state *were* successful, as was the case with Wisconsin, in particular, where the work of attracting, distributing and protecting immigrants was and is still being conducted on a high plane of efficiency.

III

These, then, are the principal attempts made in the United States to distribute immigrants. In more recent years a variety of methods have been suggested for continuing the work. In order to understand these we need first to inquire into the nature of the immigrant colony and to attempt to discover the forces which make for a *concentration* or for the *distribution* of immigrants.

The immigrant colony on first view seems highly abnormal. When closely examined, however, it is found to be the product of general social conditions and forces. The city-ward movement of the general population, the concentration of industrial establishments in certain sections, the converging of the steamship lines in the large ports, the natural desire of like for like, the dread of isolation and ostracism and the economic inability of newly arrived immigrants— all tend to create the immigrant community in the first instance and to hold it more or less loosely together once it is formed. Largely as the result of these forces in 1920, for example, ten of the fourteen million foreign born then in this country were located in cities of twenty-five hundred and over. In that same year whereas only one in two persons of the total population resided in such cities, persons of foreign birth located in them numbered nearly five out of every six. In fifty American cities the foreign born made up more than two-fifths of the population, and in twenty of these they were in the majority. The larger the city, in fact, the greater the proportion of immigrant population, New York City having in 1920 more than one-half of the population of this element.

There are conditions and forces, however, which on the other hand repel and expel immigrants from centers of segregation. The first of these inhere in the very nature of the immigrant himself. Immigrants come for the most part from rural districts, are accustomed to small community life, are comparatively young, are largely single and are for the most part unsettled with reference to their *permanent* residence; this notwithstanding the fact that as many as 90 per cent in some years state that they come to join friends or relatives. The populous city at which they debark does of course hold many of them, but those who know the situation intimately would bear out the contention that most immigrants regard the debarkation city as a sort of portal and the immigrant community a kind of halfway house to those regions or places where the opportunities for work present themselves.

In fundamental construction the immigrant colony itself is unstable. The great variety in training and outlook on the part of its component members, the wide divergence of political and religious views, the

inevitable absence of vital leadership, the weakness
of ancestral religion (the Jewish group excepted),
the instability of parental authority and the highly
controversial and unconstructive character of life—
these, playing as they do upon a comparatively limited group, tend to shake the very foundations of the
immigrant colony, to destroy whatever solidarity it
may appear to have, and to make for its instability.

For these reasons the immigrant community is
incapable of creating strong traditional memories
and values at all commensurate with those of
America at large, or strong loyalties of its
own.   The immigrant community is therefore ever
in a state of flux.   The rising generations particularly are constantly on the move.   Their contacts
with the American community arouse dissatisfaction
and discontent and these sooner or later lead them
to abandon the immigrant colony or to look forward
to doing so as soon as they can.   As Professor
Draschler puts it, in *Democracy and Assimilation*,
"The fatal disease gnawing at the vitals of the immigrant community is the 'diluted' second generation.
Silently under the roof of every immigrant home
there is going on a death struggle between two
worlds, two cultures, two civilizations.   One is fixed,
mellowed and clarified by centuries of social living
in a congenial environment; the other is as yet in-
choate, crude, halting."   Thus goaded on, the second
generation venture out more and more, intermarry-

ing with other "races" and as rapidly as opportunity permits abandon the immigrant community.

Progress in individual status tends to drive adult immigrants also out of the foreign community. "Economic progress, education, and social ambition," the Immigration Commission stated, "tend to distribute immigrants throughout a city and to hasten their absorption into the general body of residents. When the expense of moving ceases to be of great moment, when a firm economic footing is gained by the immigrant, he is likely to begin to look around for a more attractive place of residence. His ability to speak and read English, his greater familiarity with transportation facilities and the increase in his general knowledge of conditions in other parts of the city, help him in selecting a new home. . . ."

The individual immigrant is also always ready to follow economic advantage. He goes near or far, alone or with his family, under contract or aimlessly, to any part of the country, wherever the opportunity calls him. The same urge which led him to root himself out of his native village and country drives him from one city to another or from city to country. Thousands of immigrants, Grace Abbott tells in *The Immigrant and the Community*, go out of Chicago each year to "harvest Dakota crops, to build a railroad in Wyoming or Arkansas, to harvest ice in Minnesota, to pick Michigan berries, or to work on the oyster beds of Maryland." Over two-thirds of all employment agencies dealing with immigrants in Chicago offer work at distances approximating from one hundred to one thousand miles. Wherever opportunity calls immigrants will go and remain even in remote parts, so long as they are properly treated.

For all these reasons the immigrant community is in a state of constant flux. The district which yesterday was occupied by Irish to-day is inhabited by Italians and to-morrow in all probability will be the stronghold of the Pole or Hungarian. Some come in and some go out and immigrants keep "in process of incessant and most rapid migration over the face of the country, following the allurements of economic advantage and opportunities as they present themselves." The Immigration Commission also showed that in the large cities immigrant population changes much more frequently than is generally thought, and that immigrants are constantly moving on to better surroundings as soon as they are financially able to do so.

IV

It would seem, then, that the first task in developing a system of distribution would consist in recognizing and utilizing these expulsive forces. The principal problem is one of method. Coercion is advocated by some. Those who advocate forced distribution say in substance: "If they don't want to go

out of the slums, kick them out." The unwisdom of
any such procedure is so evident that it needs no
more than a passing mention. If for no other reason
compulsion should be discouraged because it is the
very thing that will build up the solidarity of the
immigrant colony and make it impregnable to large
social forces.

What, then, can be done to help immigrants
already in this country to distribute themselves?
There are virtually millions of foreign born persons
who, though they have lived in this country for
years, know little or nothing of the larger opportunities offered by the less populous centers. The Immigration Commission pointed out that thousands
return to Europe every year to invest their savings
largely because they are unacquainted with the
opportunities of particularly the newer sections of
this country. That they do not have this information is of course not their fault. The Commission
believed that much natural distribution could be
effected and many "be induced to invest their savings in this country and become permanent agricultural settlers" if ways were devised for imparting
information relative to the sparsely settled regions
of the United States.

Important as attempts to distribute immigrants
already in this country may be, of far greater impor-

tance it is to distribute those who may be admitted in the future, be they few or many.

The first question in this connection is: how to know where they are needed and how to convey the information to incoming immigrants. The Board or Commission suggested in the previous chapter would be the proper body to assemble and disseminate the requisite data. To be at all effective this information would need to be imparted to the immigrant long before he reaches this country. In fact, the further back information is carried, the more useful it will be. There was a time when to do this would have tended to stimulate emigration, but since in all probability the limit set by the 1924 law or some such definite limit will still be kept as a basis of admission, the imparting of information in the parent country would only serve to select immigrants and to direct them into those regions of this country where they would be needed.

A shipboard information service has been frequently advocated by governmental officials. Mr. T. V. Powderly, formerly chief of the Division of Information, was of the opinion that "the principal and really important duty can be performed on board the vessels." The importance of this service, especially to one whose destination is more or less still in doubt, cannot be exaggerated. It may lead him to decide to go to a section needing his labor or to suspend his judgment until he has reached the

United States and received further guidance. The difficulty arising out of the fact that immigrants, like other travelers, are often ill during the sea voyage is not as great as it may first appear, since after the second or the third day out they usually are in good health and in proportion as they approach the United States they are more eager to get information.

If previous to and during the voyage the immigrant can be helped to suspend his judgment, an exhibit at the principal ports of entrance may prove of value. Immigration officials have frequently suggested that halls be established in which the various "states, communities, or industries such as agricultural societies, coal mining associations and associations of other industries (but no individual company), should be permitted to have permanent exhibits . . . so that the admitted alien may be informed in detail as to certain industries, the wages, hours, working and living conditions, the possibility of securing employment promptly, and other matters of vital interest to the new arrival." Due precaution would need to be exercised to insure impartiality or to prevent confusing duplication of appeals. This could best be achieved under Federal supervision. In addition a government officer might act as a sort of consultant and help the immigrant to make a wise choice.

The information, whether in the form of literature or verbal advice would need to be definite and specific. Facts relative to climate, opportunities for work, methods of obtaining land should be furnished. A letter or a card of introduction to the proper government authorities in the section or locality of destination could then be given him. And upon arrival at his prospective destination the new comer should be able to secure even more specific information and advice from constituted authorities.

V

A second method to effect a distribution of immigrants and one recommended by the United States Immigration Commission is to increase the number of immigrant-receiving stations and to set a limit upon the number of aliens admitted at each port. This method, on first thought, would seem to promise but little since wherever they land, immigrants tend to drift into those sections or cities in which their compatriots reside in large numbers. But this tendency is somewhat exaggerated as we have seen. During the first few years of operation such a system would naturally not produce great results. But in time, as small deposits of immigrants were made in sparsely settled areas, such a method would inevitably lead more and more newcomers into those regions, thus creating new centers of attraction.

In fact it is precisely in this way that streams of immigrants have been directed into certain sections—as for example into parts of Wisconsin—and in time large groups have established themselves in newer and sparsely settled areas.

During the last few years fully 75 per cent of all immigrants entered through the three ports of New York, Boston and Philadelphia. At present on account of the exemption of contiguous territory from the quotas a smaller proportion enters through these points. In any case if port-apportionments could and were made, it would in time lead to a more spontaneous distribution.

Closely related to this is the suggestion made by William R. Morton, United States Vice-Consul at Athens, to the effect that the United States be divided into twelve or sixteen zones and that the annual quotas be distributed according to the size of the native and foreign born population of each zone. The consuls abroad would advise the alien from the very start whether he had or had not a place in this or the other zone. The person would understand that he was to remain in the zone to which he was originally admitted until he had become a citizen, after that he would be at full liberty to move at will. The number for each zone would be changed from time to time and therefore a much more adequate distribution be effected than at present. The proponents of this scheme recognize the element of coercion it contains, but they call attention to the fact that with governmental supervision and with emphasis placed upon proper treatment of aliens the difficulty arising out of coercion would be largely eliminated. It may be added that such a system also holds the promise of fostering a wider distribution of industrial enterprise and of promoting, thereby, still more the distribution of immigrants.

A thoroughly comprehensive distribution system would seem also to call for some form of financial aid to newly arrived immigrants. Whatever their nationality, most immigrants at the time of arrival have but small means. Often it is this lack of funds more than disinclination that prevents many from going to the sparsely settled centers. Due to the great differences in money exchange and to the cost of railway transportation in this country, the trip from the Atlantic Coast to a far off interior point is prohibitive in cost. To meet this need some kind of fare reduction would have to be devised.

Even more important is the question of giving financial aid, on a thoroughly sound business basis, to newly arrived settlers in order to permit them to get a start in farming or whatever other occupation they might go into. It is interesting to note that a system of financial aid is actually in operation in Canada and some of the South American Republics and especially in the former country is producing good results.

VI

Thus far general distribution has been dwelt upon; it remains to give a moment's attention to the subject of directing the immigrant into agriculture. The question whether immigrants should be directed into farming at all is moot. There are those who maintain that the presence of large groups of immigrants in the agricultural districts would be injurious, in that it would introduce into farm and rural life some of the social problems of the immigrant colony in the large city. The diminishing land supply, the inexperience of immigrants in the methods of American farming, the unsuccessful experience of some immigrants in American farming and their lack of capital are also cited as arguments against the distribution of immigrants on the farms. Manufacturing interests also usually oppose such a distribution obviously because it cuts down the amount of surplus labor in industrial centers.

That there is, on the other hand, a demand for additional labor on the farm in certain sections of the country is evident. According to a survey of 44 States made by the United States Employment Service in 1923, Georgia, Maine, Maryland, Massachusetts, Montana, New Jersey, North Carolina, North Dakota, Ohio, Pennsylvania, Tennessee, Utah, Washington, and Wyoming reported a definite shortage of farm labor. At the hearings held before the

House Committee on Immigration and Naturalization in 1924 various persons presented this demand before the Committee. Moreover, the South was in 1924 particularly anxious to secure farmers and insisted that agriculturalists should be given, as they were given, preference within the quotas. Later, speaking of this, Commissioner General Husband remarked: "Presumably this preference is justified, for there are some rather concrete indications that the farming population is hardly holding its own in some sections of the country. For example, only 13 per cent of the farm operators in New England are under 35 years of age and 41 per cent are 55 years of age and over. One naturally wonders what may happen in New England in the next twenty-five years." Moreover, since 1924 there has developed a definite demand for farm labor in certain sections of the country, particularly in the California and Texas cotton fields; while legislators from the South again stressed, in the 69th Congress, the need of agricultural laborers in their particular section.

It would seem, therefore, that the directing of immigrants to the farm would supply a definite demand. If this is to be accomplished, first of all there would need to be created agencies to protect immigrants in their purchase of land; state bureaus and a national clearing house for the purpose of bringing buyers and sellers together; and federal and state reclamation and colonizing agencies. A specialized information service perhaps would need to be conducted, since the average immigrant on reaching this country and even after he has been in America for some time is ignorant of the possibilities of American agriculture, and of the moral and economic advantages and the comfort and independence which present-day American country life affords.

Particularly, the immigrant, whatever his nationality, needs authoritative assistance and protection in the selection and purchase of land. Professor Richard T. Ely remarks that "If we want to bring it about that our settlers should understand our institutions and become good American citizens, we must abandon all ideas of *laissez-faire* with respect to land selection." What Wisconsin has accomplished in this regard through the supervision of the Director of Immigration and under state laws furnishes an excellent example of what may be done. That state supervises private land settlements and sees to it that the new settler is properly treated. As a result thousands of immigrants have settled in that state and have become prosperous and happy members of the community. Experience has shown that when immigrants are placed on comparatively small farms of good productivity, are given help in the initial stages of settlement in adapting themselves to American methods and sufficient time to pay for their land, in the large majority of cases they become successful and contributors to the life of the country.

The size and population composition of the rural immigrant community are of considerable social importance. The large immigrant rural colony is as undesirable as are urban colonies. The former may become virtually a foreign province, as injurious to the best interest of the country and the foreign born themselves as the Little Italy, Poland, Ghetto or Germantown of the large city. In fact the former may become even more self-sufficient, separated and segregated and therefore more anti-social than the city colony.

On the other hand the agricultural immigrant colony must be of sufficient size to constitute a small social unit or else it is bound not to succeed. Experience shows that the isolated immigrant seldom remains on the farm. Doctor E. A. Speek drawing upon the findings of wide investigation states, in *A Stake in the Land:* "The experience of private land dealers and colonization companies shows that it is not wise to settle a single immigrant family among native settlers or settlers of another nationality. Such a family becomes lonesome and sooner or later leaves the settlement. Therefore the immigrants must be settled in groups according to their nationalities. . . . Such groups ought to be from five to fifteen families each, settled in the same neighborhood among other nationalities or native settlers."

Experience also shows that in order to be successful the immigrant needs aid even after he is actually on the land. Particularly he needs the kind of guidance in land analysis, crop adaptation, coöperative buying and selling and community life which some of the more progressive states are supplying to the general farmers through their agricultural colleges. Above all, his social life must be promoted, since the very existence of the simple immigrant folk depends in no small measure upon it.

Before concluding this mention of the immigrant and agriculture, it is interesting to note briefly what the State of California is doing in the way of an experiment in land colonization. Under the Land Settlement Act of 1917 that State purchases tracts of land, clears it, prepares it for cultivation, sows the first crops, divides it into small plots, and throws it open for sale to the public. Considerable care is used in selecting the prospective buyer. The settler pays five per cent of the value of the land and forty per cent of all improvements upon taking possession and is given a period of twenty years in which to pay the remainder, on the amortization plan. The State also maintains a general, nonpaternalistic supervision of the colony, assists the farmers during the initial stages of settlement, fosters the development of social, economic, educational and coöperative buying and selling institutions and in other ways

aids the settlers in making their undertaking successful.   Although it is still in its infancy the experiment as it is being conducted at Durham and Delhi,
two of the communities built under this system, has
produced some encouraging results.   Settlers of
some ten different nationalities live and prosper side
by side and in their daily life are upholding the high
standards of American rural traditions.

CHAPTER XII

IN THE MAKING OF AMERICANS

*You were drawn across the ocean by some beckoning
finger of hope, by some belief, by some vision of a new
kind of justice, by some expectation of a better kind
of life. . . . A man does not go out to seek the thing
that is not in him. A man does not hope for the
thing that he does not believe in. . . . You dreamed
dreams of what America was to be, and I hope you
brought dreams with you. . . . Just because you
brought dreams with you, America is more likely to
realize dreams such as you brought. You are enrich-
ing us if you came expecting us to be better than
we are.—Woodrow Wilson.*

I

For more than a century of national life the people of the United States were too deeply engrossed in
the tasks of conquering a continent, exploiting its
natural resources and garnering the fruits of labor
even to think of what we now call Americanization.
In fact they were too near to the steerage to conceive of such a thing and the word "Americanization"
itself was rarely if ever used before 1900.

Then came the War! From the very first our
foreign born population showed a keen and natural
interest in the European conflict. They held meet-

ings, paraded the streets, carried on propaganda, some favoring one and others another side. But *liberty* was the central theme of all their agitations. Presumably at no time in history were so many non-natives permitted to propagate so freely within the bounds of any country as there were in the United States from the latter part of 1914 to the first months of 1917. The Irish propagated for a free Ireland, the Poles for an independent Poland, the Jews for a free Palestine, the Italians for the liberation of *Italia Irredenta*, the Serbs, Croats and Slovenes, the Armenians and other groups for the freeing of their respective countrymen from age-long enslavement.

Here, then, was America, free America incarnate, and it is decidedly to her credit that she permitted all these propagators to wage their particular battles of freedom without molestation.

In time, however, those who are always looking for an occasion to discredit immigrants began to put a special interpretation upon this more or less natural interest. They said in substance "Look! Here is proof positive that the foreign born never have been and never will be vitally concerned with *America*. Their thoughts and interests are elsewhere! See their disgraceful actions! See how stirred they are over a foreign war when they should be concerned with American affairs."

And when later the United States entered the War

they started the agitation described in Chapter V. The foreign born were charged with disloyalty. Hyphenism was discovered. Fears, distrust, incrimination cast long, dark shadows. America faced ruin! . . . unless "aliens" were Americanized.

And so the Americanization Movement came into existence. The entire country leaped into it, with that anxiety which a newly discovered danger, real or imaginary, usually evokes. Organizations of every variety turned away from their usual tasks and suddenly jumped into Americanizing efforts. Federal, state and municipal agencies, schools and churches, political parties and patriotic organizations, women's clubs, chambers of commerce, state councils of defense, "big brother" associations, social settlements, neighborhood houses, Y. M. C. A.'s and Y. W. C. A.'s, Y. M. H. A.'s and Y. W. H. A.'s, industrial and financial concerns, department stores, leagues of foreign born citizens, immigrant societies, mining engineers, groups interested in peace—all became interested in Americanizing the alien. National conventions and conferences were held, bills introduced in Congress and state legislatures, programs and policies formulated, university courses established, a dozen books, numerous pamphlets, innumerable magazine and newspaper articles published on the subject, Americanization centers opened, institutes held, teachers trained and special

Americanization days placed on the agenda of national conferences and conventions.

The movement took every conceivable force, adopted every imaginable idea. It busied itself with "Taking Uncle Sam's foster children into the family", with "putting (immigrant) mothers in the right places", Americanizing the "shut-ins", introducing the American spirit into "your city", "your town" and "your village", "making the melting pot melt." Various methods were devised. "Aliens" were made Americans by means of music and recreation, through "soap and water", athletics, motion pictures, posters and what-nots. Americanization was conceived as a "project", a "new system", a "field for college women", for "missionary" effort, an "industrial ceremonial." A technique was created for "making Americans on the railroad", for the "self-Americanization of foreign-born", and even for the "auto-Americanization by immigrant clubs in an abandoned saloon." Subsequently the American Legion and especially the Ku Klux Klan undertook to Americanize "aliens" with the hood, the club, the rope and the flaming cross.

Wherever the immigrant went, whichever way he turned; at his work, club, church, in the street, in the subway or surface car, in his home or abroad, everywhere he was confronted by "Americanization". And it is more than figuratively true that for a period

of about five years the immigrant was Americanized
from babyhood to the grave!

II

When the war and postwar scares were spent,
however, it became clear that all this Americanization
agitation was worse than futile; that, in fact, it was
producing results opposite to those intended, since
the foreign born were simply withdrawing more
deeply into immigrant colonies and were letting the
storm rage outside. Gradually the more spectacular
aspects of the movement gave way. Constructive
leaders began to take the matter in hand. Coercion
gave way to sane efforts and superficial attitudes to
fundamental thinking; and both government and private agencies began to lay deeper foundations.

As a result two different concepts of Americanization emerged, which for convenience we shall call
assimilation and *incorporation*. The two ideas have
this in common: they both aim to bring immigrants
into vital functioning in American life. They differ
however, both in fundamental idea and in the method
of achieving the end. *Assimilation*, as the word itself
denotes, aims to make the foreign born *similar* to
Americans in language, dress, customs, religion and
what not. It lays stress upon formal Americanization through naturalization. It insists that all immigrants must at all times use English and must put

away their native customs, ideas and ideals as soon as possible. In other words, *assimilation* tends to be a standardization process.

Incorporation, on the other hand, aims at a natural and normal embodying of immigrants into the whole fabric of American life. It too stresses the need of adopting the English language, American standards of living, social and political ideals and methods; it does not however demand these as prerequisites, but emphasizes them only as avenues of common and united life. Incorporation, also, grants immigrants the right to use their native languages if they wish and even encourages their teaching the foreign languages to the young and thereby building avenues of broader culture. (Further, incorporation teaches the foreign born to preserve the finer elements of their Old World cultures and to contribute them to the enrichment of American life.) Americanization is not a state that can be brought about by force, but a process in which inspiration and a natural give and take are essential; Americanization becomes an atmosphere and not an institutionalizing effort; it is a state of mind created by wholesome attitudes, fair play and normal contacts; a constant growth deriving nourishment not from sporadic or occasional propaganda, but from broad and permanent social forces; an awakening into a fuller manhood and a larger social attitude.

III

Granting that *incorporation* is the larger and more desirable concept, what forces are operative in the life of the immigrant himself and in American life which make for or militate against it? One of the forces which make for Americanization and one which is seldom recognized is found in the very idea of America which the newcomer brings with him.

To the average immigrant America is the acme of all dreams. Immigrants "new", like immigrants "old" have of course come in answer to mixed motives, the desire to improve their economic conditions probably being the most tangible of these. And yet rising above the desire for economic gain and permeating all other motives has been the desire to gain for themselves and their children the blessings of social equality, education, political and religious freedom.

Migrants of every generation, in fact, are *dreamers*, far more than seekers after bread. In lands and countries where preying rules, and men but for a starving toil unceasingly, migrant minds vision a World, far fairer than reality can give. Through the years of childhood that swiftly pass, through the years of manhood that numbly linger, they weave their far-flung fantasy; they plot and save, they pinch and starve, they look beyond the western waves their destinies to carve. For years they await to be

set free, on long life-giving quests; and when the
gates give but a hope they part with all their meager
goods, with kith and kin and loving broods; they
kiss the land that gave them birth, and with tear-
stained eyes, they set their faces toward the West,
the Westland of their hopes. In holds of ships that
rule the waves they cross the unknown seas and
patiently partake the tossings and the heaves, tossings that shall wipe all their tears. And when
against the setting sun they first behold the won-
derous Statue that marks the Gate that leads to life,
all curbings cease and out pour sight-dimming tears;
on coils of cables, on wave-wet decks they kneel and
pray, to the God of Life they kneel and pray for more
than bread can yield.

Oh, you, who wage for barring gates and you who
mock and rate, who ever fling at men's souls the
"inferiority" of their race, and you that scorn their
slothful pace to carve and hold earth's passing dust,
remember that in those holds lie dreams of life-long
years and myriad, myriad ideals; minds that suffering has refined, sturdy bodies that will toil to help
you make your paradise; a paradise of more than
steel and more than rust, where beauty shall linger
and be not crushed into dust—and loveliness and
truth and trust. They come with trust, they come
with truth, they come with beauty tinkling in their
eyes; and if you but keep them from those dreaded
cordons that make but gold and strangle life and

millions hold in walled-up towns of dreaded slums, oh, what joy they'll feel, what thrills will steel their inmost being . . . in giving and taking and in partaking of life and duty in the Land of all their dreams.

And so the subject peoples have come: the Finns, Letts, Lithuanians, Poles, Czechoslovaks, Ukranians, Roumanians, Jews, Croats, Slovenes, Serbs, Armenians and Syrians, to America they have come in search of liberty and happiness. So came the Italians, the Austrians and Hungarians, the Greeks—from lands of increasing turmoil and hunger—they came in search of a Land of peace and plenty. They looked toward America as the home of civil and religious liberty, where education was free, where toil and thrift, industry and worthy ambition could find fruition in more than animal existence. They saw in America the one place where a man, however humble he might be, might have the opportunity to achieve the best that was in him.

Let us pause to stress that this is not an argument for the open door. Not at all. It is an honest facing of facts and it is an emphasis upon the truth that this immigrant idealism may become the greatest single force for the natural Americanization of the newcomer if recognized and properly utilized.

Numerous *other forces* also impel the newcomer on the road to Americanization. His daily work, for one thing, continually drives him into the American world. There he soon discovers that a knowledge of English is a necessary prerequisite to his advancement and success. He also perceives that to adopt certain American standards is distinctly to his benefit. He presently learns also that he must have an American education if he would enter the more remunerative occupations or professions. Then there is the prestige of numbers: every influential person is an American so he *must* associate with Americans. His children attend the American school and come into contact with American ideas, and that pushes adults toward America.

So potent are these influences, in fact, that often they produce a too rapid assimilation, which in turn robs immigrants of the finer elements of Old World cultures and gives them but the veneer of American life. The desire to adopt American ways leads the Italian shoemaker to purchase a mending machine and to give up the art of making and mending shoes with care and thoroughness. The immigrant woman puts away her many-colored shawl only to wear a cheap machine-made hat. The Catholic youth yields to the pressure of his environment, becomes a Protestant, loses his love of the beautiful, the filial devotion and obedience to constituted authority, only to take on the most superficial veneer of some new-found cult. The refined Japanese girl who up to yesterday was the very embodiment of charming modesty to-day

is heard to shout to her mate in shallow, strident
notes: "Should say! That's sure keen!"

That this is not Americanization few would fail
to see and yet this is precisely what frequently takes
place in response to the forces which draw immigrants into American life.

IV

There are forces, on the other hand, which tend to
build barriers, retard and often make incorporation
impossible. The pressure of economic circumstances,
the natural desire of like for like, the repelling of the
American community, the treatment he receives in
his work—these and other influences hold the immigrant to the "colony" or drive him back whenever he
attempts to emerge.

The immigrant community becomes a city within
a city, separated by virtual walls from the larger
community of which it is a part. In that city not
only the better elements of the immigrant's native
culture are absent but also he is practically shut off
completely from the better aspects of American
life. Beyond those narrow, stifling walls the immigrant rarely goes, rarely can go, save as he goes in
and out in search of daily bread. The daily round
takes him over the same tracked ways, cutting the
confines of his little world at one and the same point
day in and day out, week in and week out, often life
in and life out. Out in that workaday world, moreover, he frequently meets with crude misunderstand-

ing, drab discourtesy, subtle or blunt abuse. Within and without these narrow worlds, exploitation hangs upon him like a dark shadow, exploitation at the hands of so-called Americans and more often perhaps by his own people. And so America becomes a gruesome reality—a promise unfulfilled. His physical America is one of noise, filth and smoke. The America of spacious skies he never sees. The better political, social and moral America he never touches. The real America is not for him to see, for him to touch and feel.

Then there come those more or less recurrent anti-immigrant agitations to drive the immigrant back—back into the segregated world. Who cannot understand how the immigrant reacts when he is made the scape-goat of every known ill in American life? At various times and places he has been made responsible for unemployment, female and child labor, the introduction of machinery, coalmine disasters, for the lack of labor organization in some quarters, and too great an organization in others, for the growth and the congestion of cities, for industrial disturbances, for political crises. Pauperism, insanity, race suicide, gambling, the continental Sunday, parochial schools, atheism, political corruption, municipal misrule, low standards of living, radicalism and every known ill of human society have been laid at the door of the immigrant.

The result? Segregation deeper and more complete! The Know Nothing and the All-American agitations of the last century played an important part in creating cohesiveness among the Irish in this country. The antiforeigners movements of the last few years have produced similar effects upon other groups. (Down to the middle of the last decade the Italian government fairly despaired of ever creating cohesion and organization among the Italians in the United States. Then came the "Black Hand" scares of 1907-1911 and the recent attacks which have stigmatized all Italians as scum of the earth. Doubtless it is in part due to this cause that the Italian group in the United States has developed a remarkable "consciousness of kind". Organizations have arisen by the score all over the country, from the national Sons of Italy and Dante Alighieri, to innumerable local societies and clubs.) Jew-baiting has likewise intensified Jewish group solidarity while the "red" scares of 1919-20 have produced a strong solidarity among the Slavs.

Nor are these all. In the reality of daily life the individual immigrant often encounters attitudes and treatment which constantly repel him. If the immigrant is polite, he is charged with being veneered or double-faced; if he is direct and positive he is called rude or "cheeky"; if he takes on American ways rapidly and becomes a citizen as soon as possible, he is considered fickle in loyalties; if he shows reluctance to relinquish his hold upon native memories and ties, he is denounced as an ungrateful guest, "a hyphenated", a menace to America; if he remains aloof and out of a sense of delicacy does not express himself on American social and political issues, he is said to lack civic interest; if he does express himself he is reminded that he is "a foreigner" and must keep his place. In poverty he is a pauper. In wealth he meets with a double envy, the envy success usually evokes and that which unsuccessful and lazy native competitors usually feel for the "damn foreigner". His frugality is said to contribute to the lowering of standards of living, his free spending is called "showy". If he clings to his kind he is "clannish", if he approaches the American community he is rebuffed and repulsed as an "undesirable".

That these are *realities* and not figments of the imagination literature bears ample evidence. These realities the immigrant encounters in his daily contacts. His enemies are many, strong, organized, entrenched, vigorous in propaganda; his friends few, weak, inarticulate and evidently powerless to lend aid in moments of greatest need.

These are the forces which repel him from the American world.

V

What we are interested in is to discover ways for removing these conditions in so far as it is humanly

possible.   Perhaps one of the greatest needs in
America to-day is that of creating a better and wider
understanding than now obtains of the immigrant
and his national and cultural backgrounds.   The
vast majority of Americans do not have much of an
idea of the wealth of culture that is deposited even
upon the humblest immigrant who sets foot upon our
shores.   A few social workers may know something
about it but the general public is woefully ignorant
of the backgrounds of immigrants, their age-long
struggles for freedom, their aims, their art, literature, music and general culture.

Then, too, it would seem as if a more honest recognition of the part the immigrant has played and is
playing in the economic life of the country would do
untold good.   "Whatever may be the country's policy
as to immigration," remarks Glenn Frank, "the recognition of the fact that thirty-five million of immigrants who have become a part of the United States
during the last hundred years *have* made vital contributions to the development of the country, would
alone serve to create a more wholesome and receptive
attitude toward those who are in the United States
at present."

What has the immigrant done?   What burdens
has he borne and is still bearing in the economic life
of this country?   Frederick Haskins makes the immigrant himself answer:

"I have shouldered my burden as the American man-of-all-work.

I contribute eighty-five per cent of all the labor in the slaughtering and meat-packing industries.

I do seven-tenths of the bituminous coal mining.

I do seventy-eight per cent of all the work in the woolen mills.

I contribute nine-tenths of all the labor in the cotton mills.

I make nineteen-twentieths of all the clothing.

I manufacture more than half the shoes.

I build four-fifths of all the furniture.

I make half of the collars, cuffs and shirts.

I turn out four-fifths of all the leather.

I make half the gloves.

I refine nearly nineteen-twentieths of the sugar.

I make half of the tobacco and cigars.

And yet I am the great American Problem.

When I pour out my blood on your altar of labor, and lay down my life as a sacrifice to your god of toil, men make no more comment than at the fall of a sparrow. . . .

My children shall be your children and your land shall be my land because my sweat and my blood will cement the foundations of the America of To-morrow.

If I can be fused into the body politic the melting pot will have stood the supreme test."

The immigrant has felled the forests, opened the land, carved the minerals, built the roads, manufactured the goods, and performed innumerable unrecorded tasks. Some maintain, as we have seen, that if not one immigrant had landed these things would still have been done. That may be true. But it still remains a matter of actual fact that most of these tasks *have* been performed by immigrants, and an honest recognition of that fact will benefit both America and the immigrant. In California there are those who are constantly stressing the indigency of the Mexicans. But what of the contribution which these dark-skinned workers are making to the riches of that state? How many million crates of oranges or grape fruit, how many tons of grapes and avocados have they picked? And perhaps it is a sad commentary upon a civilization that it gives poverty in return for such labors. Immigrants have woven the very fiber of their youthful lives into the warp and woof of this nation, until it is almost impossible to find one phase of American life which does not bear the stamp of their toil. A recognition of this fact alone would go far toward producing generous attitudes and making possible a wholesome incorporation of immigrants.

VI

In still another respect a frank recognition of fact would help greatly in the natural incorporation of the foreign born. Reference is made to the question of the use of foreign languages. We usually entertain the idea that the use of foreign languages indicates antagonism to this country.

As a matter of fact most foreign born persons generally recognize the value of a community of language and thought; but they repudiate the notion that all those who use other than the English language are disloyal. Many are the immigrants who use a non-English language and who nevertheless are most devoted Americans. If they do not learn English it is largely because of the separation in which they are obliged to live, it is because of a hard-work life, because of their age, the lack of educational opportunities and other circumstances. Even educated Americans, who live abroad for long periods, find it difficult to learn and use a new language and even when they do learn it, they often continue to use their native tongue in their daily intercourse with their countrymen. How much more natural is it, therefore, for the hardworking foreign born in this country to use their own mother tongues!

Nor do foreign-language newspapers represent disloyalty to America. The non-English press in this country is rendering a service to America which no press in English could possibly perform. With rare exceptions foreign-language newspapers are American in spirit and give non-English readers information regarding American life and world-wide events which could not be given in any other way. It is folly to assume that they foster "alien" ideas or stimulate the segregation of nationality groups in this country. The foreign-language newspaper is one of the greatest agencies of an understanding Americanism. Besides, as Durant Drake remarks (*America Faces the Future*) "to attempt to censor it [the foreign language press] is unnecessary, and would be extremely unwise, undoing our best attempts to describe America as the land of Liberty, and showing it to be actually a land of mistrust and repression."

Private foreign-language schools are likewise far from being the anti-American institutions we usually think them to be. Quite apart from the contribution they make by perpetuating some of the finer elements of Old World culture and contributing the same to the enrichment of American life, they are rendering a service which the American school, conducted in the English language, could not render, especially to adults. In California alone there are some 200 schools and 500 teachers engaged in work of this nature and their position was upheld by the recent decision handed down by the United States Supreme Court as being in keeping with the spirit and letter of the Constitution.

Writing upon this very subject, Herbert Adams Gibbons, who yields to no one in his Americanism, expresses it as his firm belief that "Education does not have to be a state monopoly. There is much to be said against abolition of private or church schools and in some cases children can be trained best in their own families by tutors or parents. We must consider avoiding the danger of destroying individuality and depriving those who want it of daily religious instruction. But the state should supervise all schools as to their curriculum, . . . provide adequate school facilities, and . . . not allow any pupils to be taught by inexperienced, untrained, or temporary teachers. If these conditions are fulfilled, we need not despair of making good Americans out of all the immigrants who are already here." (*America's Place in the World.*) In any event what is needed is tolerance and understanding, rather than suppression and wholesale condemnation.

VII

The thoughtful reader has probably noticed that throughout the preceding pages *attitudes* rather than institutions have been stressed. This has been done on the assumption that far above what the school, the church or the club may be able to do toward the incorporation of the immigrant, far above classes, meetings and propaganda, the immigrant will be influenced more by the *treatment* he receives in his daily intercourse with Americans and especially at his work than by anthing else. Well may the United States Bureau of Education believe that "The immigrant is becoming either Americanized or anarchized by every experience which he undergoes, every condition to which he is subjected. Americanization is in a measure the problem of the school. But it is also a matter of prevention of exploitation, of good housing, of Public Health, of clean milk for babies, of adequate wages, of satisfactory industrial conditions, of the spirit of neighborliness between Americans, old and new. Everything that touches the immigrant's life is an instrument for his Americanization or the reverse."

When this concept of Americanization prevails we shall "invest this attempt of ours to build a superior social order with a richness of meaning that will force us to see that Americanization is something more than saluting the Goddess of Liberty, learning the English language, memorizing the Constitution, and forgetting one's racial and cultural heritage." (Glenn Frank.) Then we shall learn that Americanization is not something that we are to *do* to the immigrant, but that it is rather a noble national adventure in which we invite the immigrant to coöperate. Then the immigrant himself will be raised above merely doctrinal tests and static political creeds, and he will know that "he is receiving the inspiring opportunity to share in the creative task of building a new and superior social order."

CHAPTER XIII

AND STILL THEY MOVE

Man is not destined, like plants and most animals, to remain in the soil in which he was born; an instinct, an inborn urge, uniting in some with a spirit of adventure and curiosity, drives him forth in search of wealth and well-being, and to extend his activity and influence to the farthest bounds of his power.—*Calvo.*

I

ON September 14, 1924, the immigrants on Ellis Island had gone to their evening meal. Seven aliens, however (two Spaniards, one Italian, one Mexican, one Portuguese, one Russian and one of unknown nationality), chose rather to seek other food, and, plunging into the channel which separates Ellis Island from the New Jersey coast, they started to swim toward the Land of Promise. With grim irony their course turned toward *Liberty Port*, New Jersey. In mid stream, however, three of them became exhausted. One was reported drowned. Two were dragged back to Ellis Island by one of their number. The rescuer and the remaining three finally gained *Liberty Port*, but presently found themselves behind prison bars and later were deported.

Were this but a singular incident it might be buried in the pages of a day, as having no particular social importance, and forgotten. But it appears to be not a singular incident. In various portions of the earth men seem to be taking all kinds of hazards in order to liberate themselves from stifling conditions and influences. In Europe and Asia, men, women and children are moving with the eagerness which man employs when he strives to preserve life itself. International Labor Office records covering nineteen countries alone show that during a period of three years (1921-1923) more than two and a half millions of persons (2,586,782) moved from one country to another, or from one continent to a second. In Europe large numbers seem to be virtually standing upon the shores looking eagerly for some new home. D. Christie Tait, British Representative of the International Labor Office states that at the beginning of the present fiscal year there were in the United Kingdom 80,000 applications for visas for the United States, while the quota is only 34,007; in Poland 75,000 applications and a quota of 5,982; in Italy 12,000 and 3,845; in Czechoslovakia 40,000 and 3,073 and so on. "Moreover, it was estimated that there was a potential demand, represented by persons who had not actually made any application, at least as large as the 'reported demand' represented by written applications." (Journal of Royal Institute of International Affairs, January 1927.)

In the face of increasing restriction upon the freedom of movement migrants are flinging themselves
against all kinds of obstacles, devising every conceivable means, taking every possible chance, staking
their all, jeopardizing even life itself in search of
larger opportunities. Some disguise thier nationality; some pose as agriculturists (usually on preferred
lists); some knowingly or ignorantly move behind
false passports, or without any passports whatso-
ever; one woman is reported to have bought a husband in the hope that through the purchased nationality she might enter the New World.

And just beyond the confines of the United States
thousands are reported to be eagerly watching for
an opportunity to enter this country. Two hundred
thousand persons—Spanish, Chinese, Jews, Japanese
—were said to be stranded on the Island of Cuba in
1924-25; in Havana's most unsanitary section alone
some ten to twelve thousand of them were huddled
together, forming colonies where their kind have
never been before. In Jamaica some ten thousand
were similarly stranded, while groups of Jews, Jews
from Austria, Germany, Russia, Roumania, Bohemia,
made their way into Mexico to await the time "until
admission to the United States is arranged."

Coming even closer, we see the drama of life and
death being enacted upon the very boundaries of the
United States. Since the enactment of the restrictive
laws migrants have been devising every imaginable

means in their attempts to enter the zone of abundance. They sail in little schooners and fishing smacks; cross rivers in fragile boats; make their way over snowbound passes, over ice covered rivers and lonely deserts. They swim, crawl on hands and knees or "fly". They pay fabulous sums—doubtless the savings of years—to be carried across. Thousands enter as seamen, hundreds as stowaways. Some even travel half around the globe, enduring unheard of hardships in the hope of entering America. Six Chinese are reported to have come the entire distance from Hongkong to Brooklyn, New York, packed in cases, arriving half famished and dying—two actually died. "Two dozen Japanese, rainsoaked and half starved and miserable were discovered one stormy morning not long since on a barren island off the Florida coast." One group of aliens made a dash across the Niagara River and all but lost their lives as their boat skirted the rim of Niagara Falls. One family from Hungary with little babies in their arms undertook to run the gauntlet of the cold and the dangers of air holes as they tried to cross the ice-covered Detroit River.

II

Viewed in the light of man's tireless striving to find a fuller existence these happenings assume a deep significance. They symbolize that vast human drama we call migration; a drama whose numberless actors originating in many parts of the globe go to play their act of life and death upon the borderlands between the Old and the New Worlds.

And theirs is not a "play" but the real struggle of life itself. For it is not "sport" that leads them to pull out the roots of nativity, break ties, part with home and kin, and place in jeopardy all they are and all they possess. It is rather necessity which impels them onward; need, inflexible and unbending, that expels them out of their native haunts and hamlets and draws them toward those portions of earth which give a promise of a fuller life.

Nor is this a new phenomenon. Men of every known race, practically from every portion of earth, have moved throughout recorded history, now simply roving as nomads, now led by tribal leaders; sometimes conquering with the sword, more often colonizing by the arts of peace. In recent centuries they have been driven by religious and political persecutions or by simple economic need. And they have moved, moved *en masse,* in small groups, by families and as individuals. They have moved in the face of apparently insurmountable obstacles. They have scaled craggy and snow covered mountains, crossed rivers, spanned continents, traversed once-impassable oceans. In this manner the human race has spread from its original habitats to the four corners of the earth, forming races and sub-racial groups, giving birth to new states, transmitting institutions, mobilizing and utilizing the labor and productive forces of the race.

With the development of transportation of the last century, with the industrialization of new countries, the dissemination of knowledge, the growth of democratic ideas, the partial emancipation of the working classes, the breaking down of the self-sufficiency of localities, the movement of peoples has greatly accelerated, and men have moved at a rate and with a rapidity probably greater than ever experienced before; they have gone forth

> "To add more miles to the tally
>   Of grey miles left behind,
> In quest of that one beauty
>   God put [them] here to find."

Transportation facilities have distributed population as well as products; have carried peoples to the food as well as food to the peoples. As marked inequalities have arisen between places, not only necessities have been imported from lands having a surplus, but also portions of the population have been exported or imported; and the tendency to equalize the conditions of men has become world-wide and the migratory movement a world problem. It is estimated that as many as seventy-five millions left Europe alone during the last one hundred years, of whom 37,000,000 have come to the United States.

Nor may we look for a cessation or even any appre-

ciable permanent diminution of the general movement. Such figures as exist indicate that the annual
average of oversea emigration from thirteen European countries alone amounted to 1,368,367 in
1911-13 and that total migration amounted to about
five millions a year. Reports from nineteen countries
show that more than two and a half million persons
migrated from one country or continent to another in
the years 1921-23, that oversea emigration from thirteen European countries amounted to an annual average of 685,217 during the four years 1920-23. And
when repatriation and surreptitious migration are
considered the movement assumes considerable proportions and it is possible that when the postwar
economic crisis has spent its power we may see an
even greater movement than that of the prewar
years.

So long as conditions differ from country to country and continent to continent in all probability
men will still continue to move. Difference in the age
of countries, in climate, density of population, the
presence of mineral and other natural resources, the
degree of industrial development, the rate of population increase, national ideals and aspirations, the
stage of civilization—all these and numerous other
differences tend to pull up men's roots and to set
them moving. Some move within a given country,
some between one nation and another and some venture out across oceans to distant continents. Unless

basic conditions change or are changed we must expect a continued flow.

III

It is worthy of note that governments have at various times attempted to control both the outward and the inward movement of peoples. It will be recalled that England of the seventeenth and eighteenth centuries, for example, endeavored to prevent its subjects from leaving; and the colonists complained of that fact in their Declaration of Independence. Germany under Bismarck made similar attempts and in more recent times also Sweden, Denmark and Norway. Italy since the nineties of the last century has attempted to restrict the outward movement of its population and Czechoslovakia even to-day places restriction upon the emigration of certain classes, particularly agriculturists.

Governments have endeavored to control emigration chiefly because the loss of their population was not so agreeable as it at first appeared. Emigration tended to increase the disproportion between the sexes; to take away the most active and vigorous and to leave behind large portions of the very young and the very old; it tended to rob a country of skilled workers, brought up to maturity at great expense.

But great difficulties have been encountered, difficulties due chiefly to the highly human character of migration. Emigration countries have had to determine how they could *force* their people to remain within their territories without being obliged to build formidable armies for the purpose of compelling their subjects to stay in zones of starvation. They have been obliged to face questions such as these: Of the numerous candidates presenting themselves, whom should they permit to leave and whom force to remain? By what means should they check clandestine emigration, guard the channels of exit, prevent the work of promoters, the dissemination of false information, the fabrication of false documents, when officials, guards and armies alike are themselves of the starving or oppressed multitude and gladly bid a god-speed to those who *can* go? In the face of the resistless urge, driving men on in search of better living conditions, governments have been practically helpless in stemming the *outward* flowing tide of men—a fact rarely recognized in immigration countries.

And the wonder is not so much that governments have failed, but rather that they have done so well in controlling the outward flow. There is every reason to believe that, considering the conditions obtaining, a country like Japan has accomplished miracles in this respect. Nor is it difficult to understand why an enlightened nation like Norway has frankly admitted the utter uselessness of prohibiting emigration by arbitrary and artificial means.

Nor have receiving countries been spared from grave difficulties as they have attempted to stem the *inward* flow. State after state: Belgium, Germany, Fiume, has sought to bar the poor, the physical, moral, and, more recently, the political undesirable, and to restrict the number of laborers coming in, but with practically no tangible results.

The United States in particular, as we have seen, for nearly half a century has directed great energies to endeavors to control the quality and quantity of immigration; first barring paupers, criminals and mental defectives; then prohibiting the entrance of laborers under contract; later adding the illiterate, the politically and morally undesirable to the excluded classes; and finally by the laws of 1921 and 1924 it set definite limits to the number admissible and excluded certain sub-"racial" groups in part and specific "races" entirely.

The difficulties attending these efforts are too well-known to need extended comment. Undoubtedly *some* undesirables have been kept out, but it is doubtful whether the results have been at all commensurate with the energies expended. The size of the stream in all probability has also been kept smaller than it might have been otherwise and yet, as we have seen from the facts and figures presented in Chapter Six, it appears as if the volume of net immigration has remained practically unaltered, the figures ranging around 550,000 for the years of greatest restriction as well as for the period previous to the War when immigration was practically unrestricted.[1]

IV

Various methods are advocated to obviate these difficulties and assume a firmer control of migration. In the United States aside from general restriction principally three methods are suggested: strengthening the border patrol, placing the Western Hemisphere on the quota basis, and registration and deportation of aliens.

There are large groups in the United States who, still adhering to the mechanistic concept of migration, seem honestly to believe that the migration flow will be arrested by building a higher protective dam than we now have. The 68th and 69th Congresses appear to have had this faith. They appropriated one million dollars a year in addition to other sums for the sole purpose of strengthening the border patrol. At the close of the fiscal year 1925 there were approximately 450 persons in the United States patrol service made up principally of former Army

[1] This statement applies particularly to the period previous to 1924. The law of that year has not been sufficiently long in operation to warrant sound conclusions.

or Navy men, who on foot, by motor vehicle and by boat patrolled 2,288,000 miles of border, questioned or investigated 1,252,379 persons and engaged in many other similar activities. In the spring of 1926 some of these patrol officers even invaded cities of Southern California and promiscuously arrested many Mexicans in an endeavor to "round up" persons who had entered surreptitiously. In each successive annual report the Commissioner General of Immigration suggests the need of increased appropriations in order to strengthen the present cordon and build new lines of defense.

There are others, however, who consider this not a true solution. They believe that it is not a matter of holding a Thermopylæ pass against a small organized army, but rather the guarding of nine-thousand miles of border against *individual* particles of human dust blown toward America by the urge of life itself. The United States Secretary of Labor is reported to have said that "If we had the Army on the Canadian border and on the Mexican border, we couldn't stop them; if we had the Navy on the water-front, we couldn't stop them." In fact not even a Chinese wall, nine thousand miles in length and built over rivers and deserts on mountains and along the seashores, would seem to promise a permanent solution.

A second remedy proposed is that we shall control immigration by placing all contiguous territory,

Canada, Mexico, the countries of Central and South America, et cetera, on a quota basis. The natives of these countries, we have seen, if otherwise admissible are now permitted to enter irrespective of quotas and for justice's sake perhaps they should be placed under the quota. But to place them under quota restrictions, promising as it may seem, would only serve to further complicate the problem. For if considerable difficulty is now being experienced in preventing immigrants from entering surreptitiously through contiguous territory, what results can possibly be expected from this move? These countries might, of course, themselves adopt restrictive immigration laws, but this is a very remote possibility. Canada, in fact is systematically attracting immigrants. So it would seem as if large deposits of European immigrants would still be made in those territories, with the result that these would continue to press against the United States borders. With contiguous territory placed on a quota basis the pressure would probably be increased. And if it is difficult at present to protect the borders and if immigration officials find it impossible to discover who is and who is not an immigrant as, for instance, the ferry at Detroit plies back and forth between Canada and the United States during rush hours, how will the placing of contiguous territory under the quota possibly do other than complicate the problem?

A third solution proposed is that all aliens in the

United States be registered once a year. Under the guise of "school registration" and "naturalization registration" various proposals have been made for the forced registration of all aliens. The Secretary of Labor has advocated this and President Coolidge has more than once hinted at the possible necessity of adopting this expedient. By this method the seven million aliens now residing in this country would be required to register each year. Indirectly this is control of immigration, since it is usually proposed that those found without credentials of legal entry would be subject to apprehension and deportation.

"Found without credentials"? But the problem is how "found"? This would necessitate, aside from the border patrol, another little army to patrol the streets of every city. The expense entailed would be enormous; the problem of personnel tremendous. In addition, the question is: what would be done with those apprehended without proper credentials? Deport them? But suppose that thousands are so found? What could the United States do with them? The Commissioner General of Immigration stated that it would cost half a million dollars to deport "between two and three thousand" Chinese seamen who were known to be in this country illegally in 1924. How much would it cost to apprehend and deport scores of thousands? Such a method appears objectionable from still another point of view, in that it would be but a step in the direction of the

espionage system which would, perchance, produce
evils far more fatal to the life of American democracy than those it would seek to cure.

V

It would seem as if more constructive methods
must be devised and employed for even a partial solution of the problems of regulating migration. Since
the war the question has more than once made an
appearance in the councils of nations: at the Peace
Conference, in connection with the discussions on the
Protocol for the Pacific Settlement of International
Disputes, as well as in connection with the question
of extending the activity of the International Labor
Office in finding employment for workers other than
refugees.

A number of nations have, in recent years, entered
into agreements which seek to assume international
regulation of migratory movements.

Several countries have adopted commercial and
other treaties containing provisions respecting emigration and immigration. The Covenant of the
League of Nations, also, laid down conditions regarding the movement of laborers, and several treaties
adopted under that Covenant make provisions for
the organization of international agencies for an
international control of migration.

In addition, a number of nations have entered into
special treaties on emigration and immigration.

Agreements of this nature have been entered into
between France and Poland, France and Italy, Bulgaria and Greece, France and Czechoslovakia, Italy
and Luxembourg, Austria and Poland and Italy and
Brazil, all in the years 1919 to 1921. Several other
agreements have been reached of which perhaps the
best example is that between Italy and Switzerland
of February 1927. These treaties and agreements
establish the principles of equal wages, living and
labor conditions for all workers, native or foreign,
and make provisions for the prevention of recruiting
of foreign workers who might become injurious to
native workers.

Finally the growing recognition that migration is
a world-wide problem has led to a discussion of the
matter at international conferences. Before the war
no conference covering this subject was held. In
1919 the International Emigration Commission was
created under the auspices of the League of Nations,
with representatives from seventeen nations, for the
purpose of bringing about coördination and coöperation in migration matters. In 1921 this Commission
met in Geneva and adopted resolutions. In May
1924 representatives of fifty-seven nations met in
Rome, at the invitation of Italy, in an International
Conference on Emigration and Immigration. For a
period of three weeks the delegates discussed the
principal international aspects of migrations. The
resolutions adopted, which have come to be known

as *The Migrant's Charter,* define and place limits upon the right to emigrate and immigrate; call for international coöperation in securing sanitary conditions, moral protection to women and minors, and insurance against sickness or death in the course of the voyage and in foreign countries; and recommend that the nations act jointly in the gathering and in the disseminating of information relative to opportunities, conditions, laws, et cetera, and in rendering migrants legal and judicial aid. *The Migrant's Charter* recommends also the standardization of travel documents, equality of wages, treatment and working conditions, and the encouragement of the family as the unit of migration.

It will be readily seen, of course, that these movements offer but superficial remedies and that society must one day go much further. World society must face the questions of raw materials, climates and contours, division of labor, unused lands and many other similar problems.

The largest question which must sooner or later be raised is that which the late James Bryce frankly asked but a few months before his death. He was discussing the *Forces and Influences Making for War or Peace* at Williamstown, when he asked: "Has a State any right to forbid entrance to harmless foreigners of any particular race or to make the color of their skin a ground for exclusion?"

Two doctrines, Bryce pointed out, have been

advanced in reply to this question: "One, which found favor two generations ago, held that *prima facie* every human being has a natural right to migrate from any one part of the world to any other, the world being the common inheritance of mankind, and that only very special conditions can justify the exclusion of any particular race or class of men. The other doctrine is that each State is at all times free to exclude any foreigners from entering any part of its territory, and that no ground for complaint on the part of any other States arises from such exclusion, unless where a foreign State claims that its own citizens are being discriminated against either in breach of treaty rights or in a way calculated to wound its national susceptibilities."

In practice, "The White Races," continued Bryce, "have used both as each suited their convenience." But "opinion has latterly tended to recognize the right of absolute exclusion by the State which owns the territory; so far at least as that right is not offensively exercised. This view has been justified in the case of some of the colored races by two practical arguments: One is that as friction cannot be prevented from arising between the colored immigrants and the whites among whom they come, it is safer they should not come at all. The other is that the growth of a mixed race produced by the union of whites and persons of color raised difficult political as well as social problems. . . .

"But the problem might become serious if any people were to persist in their policy of exclusion so far as to keep practically empty vast areas too hot to be cultivated by white labor, and into which races of another color would like to pour the overflow of their constantly increasing population.   There is no international authority entitled to intervene, but if the problem should ever become acute, it may have to be solved by a public opinion of the world—a public opinion which does not now exist but which ought to exist—and solved with a view to the benefit of mankind as a whole, a thing not yet recognized as constituting a paramount aim which international policy ought to recognize." (*International Relations*, pp. 126-129.)

VI

World opinion is, however, definitely and increasingly coming to recognize this "paramount aim"; at least it perceives the necessity of international coöperation in any attempt to solve the more practical problems connected with migration.

A considerable portion of the American public, on the other hand, seems as yet disinclined to accept the international view of the matter.   Due in part perhaps to our geographic position and our prosperity, and in part to the immediacy of social problems resulting from the great flow of immigration, our legislators, especially, have been inclined to look upon immigration as a purely mechanical movement, more or less artificial, susceptible to easy control and domestic in character. The phrase "immigration is a purely domestic matter" has been repeated so often, that we actually have come to believe it to represent the fact. Legislators, especially in connection with the parliamentary discussions of 1924, defended the doctrime with passionate zeal and fervor. The United States is said to have kept out of the League of Nations in part because it wished to avoid an international discussion of migration. It is probable also that the same motive was behind the famous fifth reservation which for the time being at least is keeping the United States out of the Permanent Court of International Justice.

There is a body of public opinion in the United States, however, which takes the larger view. It recognizes that there are phases of migration which are domestic, that a nation has the right to determine what kind and how many people it wishes to admit. But, many think, coöperation with other nations in carrying out even such wishes would produce more satisfactory results, since the movement entails so many factors which are highly human, strictly international and not susceptible to easy control.

As early as 1907 United States legislators recognized the necessity of such international coöperation. Section 29 of the law of that year authorized the

President of the United States to call international conferences and to appoint special commissions to make investigations abroad, a provision which was reënacted in the 1917 law. The Immigration Commission likewise recommended the appointment of a commission to work out legislation with the leading countries of Europe.

Professor Jeremiah W. Jenks, who for many years has been a close student of immigration, voiced the sentiment of this body of opinion when he said before the United States Senate Committee on Immigration in 1921: "Our immigration question is a great international problem and it is becoming more and more an internatioal problem all the time. . . . It is decidedly an advantage, practically a necessity, that we deal with foreign Governments in connection with this question of immigration. . . . That would in no way imply that we in any sense had changed our policy as regards the first principle that was laid down here, that our great task is to maintain the standards of living and to promote the standards of living of the great mass of our wage-earning class."

"There can be no true solution of our immigration question," Edwin Goldman pointed out in 1923, "which does not provide for the mutual interests of the nations concerned. . . . If we followed European countries and made immigration treaties we should be forming 'untangling' alliances, providing more

protection to American labor than the present contract labor law. . ."

And the National Industrial Conference Board
has expressed it as its view that "the immigration
problem is essentially a human problem, international in scope and involving deep and far-reaching
racial and social questions. It is clear . . . that a
wise, comprehensive and humane national immigration
policy cannot be based exclusively on the consideration of any immediate, special, local or purely economic aspect of the problem, but must be developed
out of broad, far-sighted and scientifically-grounded
views of national and international social and economic progress and human welfare."

VII

To what extent the latter view is gaining ground
in the United States is difficult to say. The people
of this country as a whole abstractly seem to believe
in the principles of peace, economic expansion and
coöperation. And yet in practice they adhere to isolation, especially in governmental relations with other
nations. The *people* of the United States, as *people*
are increasingly coöperating in all kinds of unofficial
enterprises with the peoples of other countries, and
it may be that herein lies the hope of the future. It
may be that that interpeople coöperation will one
day make possible constructive international efforts
of all kinds and will make possible also a constructive
immigration policy, such as is suggested in Chapter

X, which while safeguarding the interests of this country will at the same time consider the international phases of the matter.

Much of the future of the nations, indeed much of the future of civilization may depend upon whether the United States will adopt the larger point of view. For migrations may be expected to continue for some time to come.

The forces which lead men to move are, we repeat, as deep as life itself. Men do not pull up the roots of nativity, break the ties of home and kin, and place in jeopardy all they are and all they own, even life itself, for the mere joy of doing so. Basic conditions expel them out of some countries and draw them toward others; conditions which act upon men as natural forces do upon the elements. As the sun pours down its intense rays upon a snow-covered mountain and the snows melt, waters gather into rivulets and streams and these, joining, move toward the ocean. The river may be diverted in part, it may be dammed, but down pour the waters. Some of them will accumulate behind dams, but the waters which follow will flow over them. At certain times of the year they will flow more than at others, one year more than a second, but still they will move, at about the same rate of speed and with approximately the same volume year in and year out, *unless* the generating conditions somehow alter.

So with the human stream! As long as conditions make deposits of poverty and hunger upon the human body and mind, so long men may be expected to move. As the knowledge of new lands arises to cast its rays of hope upon them, they will move, move over the precipices of shattered homes and broken ties. Some will be held back, but the many will run over the dams into those places which promise the good life. Need goads them on. The hope of satisfying that need draws them toward new worlds. Unless the conditions which generate the movement are mitigated or removed, the human stream will continue in its flow. It will flow in response to differences in birthrates, density of population, economic pressure, social, political and religious conditions; and men *will* move in the face of death in search of life.

The United States stands at the very center of this movement. Merely to bar her gates, to build further lines of defense or to attempt to ward off such migrants as are not wanted, desirable and expedient as it may be in the immediate sense, will only serve to postpone the larger solution of the problem. If the United States, on the other hand, should join hands with other nations it is not at all impossible that world society may find a way out of some of the intricate problems arising from the migratory movement.

VIII

A consideration of the underlying forces, the ever

varying conditions, the changes in attitudes, the
ideals, hopes and fears of human beings—American
and foreign born alike—have led to the writing of the
story contained in the preceding pages. The story
is so vast in its scope, so human, vital and throbbing
that only the fringes of it have been touched. The
aim has been to interpret rather than to propagate
this or the other idea, to feel after a basic understanding of the facts and forces at work. And even
deeper, perhaps, there lies a desire to hold on to the
larger, world-wide significance of America. Underlying all is the dream—vain, foolish dream some will
doubtless call it—that reaches after a country above
national and racial antipathies, a country in which
are exercised "those more rare and noble courtesies
which spring from liberality of opinion"; the dream
of a world in which men of all nations may one day
be moved by the spirit of the great American patriot
William Lloyd Garrison

> The world is my country,
> My countrymen are all mankind.

INDEX

Abbott, Grace, 236

Act To Encourage Immigration, 29

Admission, 212; criteria in colonies, 8 ff.; effects of colonial system, 9 ff.; negative principle, 213; numerical, 220 ff.; positive principle, 213; standards, 213 ff.

Advertising, 37

Agitations, anti-immigrant, 24 f.; 88 f.; anti-Japanese, 169 f., 172; effects, 261 ff.

Agricultural colony, 245 ff.

Agricultural laborers, need for in South, 245; preferred in 1924 Law, 145 f.

Aldrich, T. B., 41

Alien Land Laws, 167

Alien Law, 24; repealed, 26

America, for Americans, 25, 55; governments fail in winning, 4 ff.; immigrants' dream, 256 f.; significance to laborers, 17 f.

American Army, composition, 81 f.

American capital abroad, 200, 202 f.

American Fathers, 189, 190, 211

American Federation of Labor, 87, 108; demands suspension, 86

American-Japanese Society of Tokio, 181

American Legion, 89, 107

American nationality, spirit, 206

American public opinion, 171, 292; rejects international view, 289

American Red Cross, 106

American university heads object, 180 f.

Americanization, 250 ff.; barriers, 260; Black Hand scares, 262; forces hindering, 260; forces making for, 256 f., 258 f.; immigrant communities, 260; immigrants' ideals, 256 ff.; larger concept, 256, 270; many forms, 252 f.; previous to War, 250; World War agitation, 250 f.

Anderson, Benjamin M., 199

Anglo-Saxons, 114, 192

Antecedents, emphasized, 189

Anti-immigrant agitations, 24 f., 29, 52, 88 f.; results, 261 f.

Anti-Japanese movement, 169 f., 172

Antipathy, national, 131 f.

Armenian refugees, 105 ff.; organizations and persons favoring admission, 107 ff.; persons opposed, 110 f.; refused admission, 112

Arthur, C. A., 34

Artificial restriction, 125